EPISCOPI VAGANTES
AND THE
ANGLICAN CHURCH

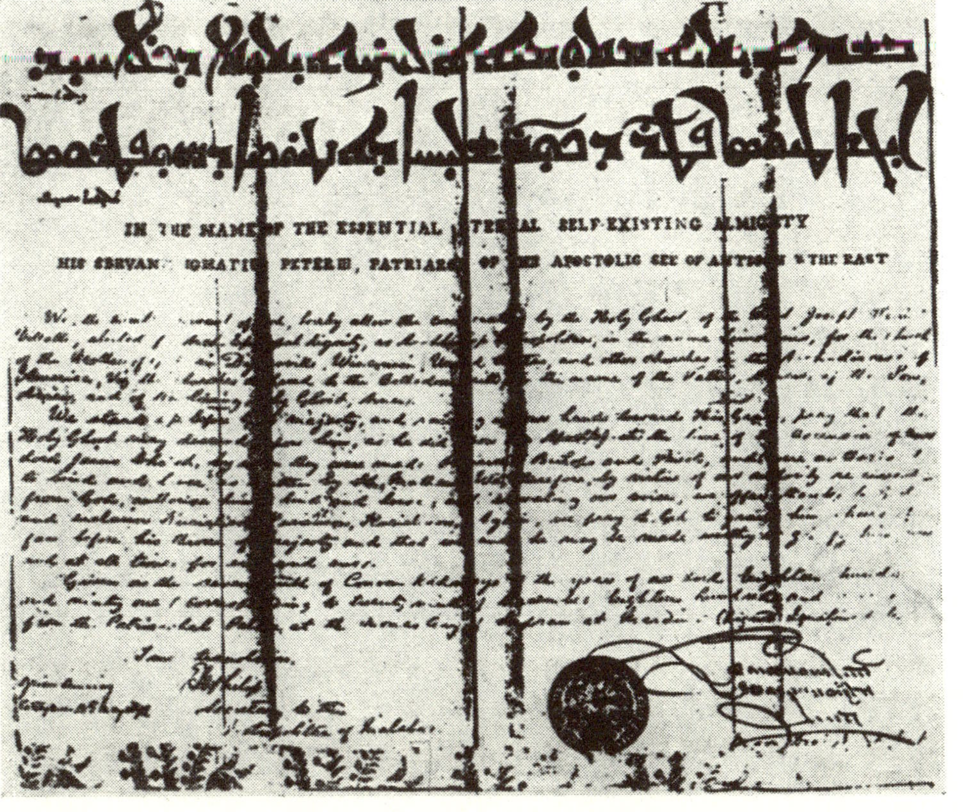

IN THE NAME OF THE ESSENTIAL ETERNAL SELF-EXISTING ALMIGHTY

HIS SERVANT IGNATIUS PETER III, PATRIARCH OF THE APOSTOLIC SEE OF ANTIOCH & THE EAST

Alleged Original Translation of the Bull of Ignatius Peter III of Antioch, for the Consecration of J. R. Vilatte.

[Frontispiece.

EPISCOPI VAGANTES
AND THE
ANGLICAN CHURCH

BY

HENRY R. T. BRANDRETH

the apocryphile press
BERKELEY, CA
www.apocryphile.org

apocryphile press
BERKELEY, CA

Apocryphile Press
1700 Shattuck Ave #81
Berkeley, CA 94709
www.apocryphile.org

First published in 1947 by the Society for Promoting Christian Knowledge. First Apocryphile Press Edition, 2006. Reprinted by permission of the Society for Promoting Christian Knowledge.

For sale in the USA only. Sales prohibited in the UK.
Printed in the United States of America

ISBN 0-9771461-7-0

CONTENTS

APPENDICES

LIST OF ILLUSTRATIONS

PREFACE

This small book had its origin in a Report I was asked to prepare some years ago on the subject of *episcopi vagantes.* While gathering the information on which that Report was based, it became obvious that most Anglicans had not even heard of the existence of such people. It seemed, therefore, that some general account of the subject might be of interest, and it was clearly desirable that those charged with the administration of the Church should have some compendium of information, which might be of service should they ever have to deal with any of the persons of whom this book speaks.

The study of that light-hearted trafficking in holy things, which characterises so many of the *episcopi vagantes,* cannot fail to be a painful one. It is, none the less, a study which ought to be undertaken, since much of the harm done by these misguided men has been due to ignorance, on the part of Churchmen, of their true aims and position. I hope I have made it clear in the pages which follow that all *episcopi vagantes* are not tarred with the same brush. Since undertaking the study of the movements which they represent I have come into contact with a number of them, and for some, however much I may disagree with the position which they have adopted, I have come to cherish a personal liking and respect, and these, I feel sure, will wish me to tell the truth as I see it, however unpalatable to them that truth may be.

Slight as this book is, it could not have been written without the generous help of a number of persons. I owe my introduction to the subject, in any full sense, to Canon J. A. Douglas, and throughout the six years in which I have been studying it he has been a master guiding me in right paths; to him this book owes its origin and much of its contents, and that is but one of many reasons I have to offer him a tribute of gratitude. I am also indebted to Dr. A. J. Macdonald, who read the typescript and made valuable suggestions. Lord Lang, when Archbishop of Canterbury, graciously allowed me access to files of papers relating to Bishop Mathew, and I am indebted to the present Archbishop of Canterbury for the same privilege. For help at particular points I am indebted to the Archbishop of Utrecht, the Bishop of Chichester, the Bishop of Los Angeles, Dr. C. B. Moss, Dr. Floyd W. Tomkins, the Rev. Maurice Bévenot, S.J., the Ven. John E. Culmer, Mr. F. Brittain and many more; I am very grateful to them. I have also courteously been permitted to examine the copy of Bishop Mathew's Register which, so far as I can judge, is undoubtedly in his handwriting. Miss M. V. Wallace, of the Church of England Council on Foreign Relations, has given me constant help at all points.

H. R. T. B.

FOREWORD

By

THE REV. CANON J. A. DOUGLAS, PH.D., D.D.
Formerly Hon. General Secretary of the Church of England Council on Foreign Relations

In sum and substance this book is a *Who's Who* of the *episcopi vagantes* who have appeared in Anglo-American lands during the past sixty years. It was in 1939 that, as he states in his Preface, we appealed, for practical reasons, to Fr. Brandreth to undertake its compilation. We were able to supply him with a considerable mass of material, and he was already equipped with no small knowledge of the obscure field which we asked him to investigate. During the past seven years he has worked with singular assiduity and discrimination at that investigation. The result is this book, which of its kind is archetypal, and by which he has earned the gratitude, not only of officials such as myself, but of the Anglican Communion in general, and in particular of the student of the Church life of our own times, as indeed of the theologian and of the ecclesiastical historian.

I estimate our debt to Fr. Brandreth for this book very highly, because of the need which it so well supplies.

An *episcopus vagans*, i.e. a bishop who, without canonical authority, intrudes himself of his own will into the jurisdiction of other bishops, is no modern phenomenon. But in all history, so far as I am aware, until sixty years ago no *episcopus vagans* had ever been more than a minor and isolated freak or nuisance.

Of the *episcopi vagantes* named by Fr. Brandreth, some have been of patent sincerity and simplicity of life. Others have been megalomaniacs or paranoiacs, and often of ill-repute. But none has been the leader of a schism other than of a minute and transient kind from any church, nor has any been distinguished for scholarship or for impact upon the thought of our time.

They have had a single characteristic in common. One and all have declared themselves to be possessed of valid episcopal orders derived from an historic Church, the apostolic succession of which is accounted unchallengeable by Western theologians. And though their power to do so has been repudiated by that Church, each and all of them have proceeded to confer what they claimed to be valid episcopal and other orders upon men who did not belong to that Church.

If it be asked why, whereas none appeared in England during the seventeenth and eighteenth centuries, a sporadic and prolific crop of *episcopi vagantes*, conferring 'valid orders' broadcast, appeared in England and America during the past hundred years, the answer is that until the middle of the nineteenth century no one except a few controversialists was interested in the validity or invalidity of Anglican Orders. Whatever else was challenged in the seventeenth century, the old concept of the identity of the Church and nation remained everywhere axiomatic. Two English Churches were as unthinkable as two English nations. The struggle which convulsed England was as much ecclesiastical as political. Its bilateral issue was as to whether or not the English nation should be ruled by a monarchy with right divine, and the English Church be ruled by bishops in the apostolic succession. As James I put it: "No Bishop; no King." While the Puritan was threatening to extirpate the English episcopate by force of arms, who could trouble his head with the secondary issue as to whether, in the days of Elizabeth, Archbishop Parker's consecration had been valid or not?

To be fair, the papalist controversialist of the seventeenth century denounced Anglican Orders on much the same grounds as his successor of to-day denounces them—viz., for breach of continuity in the laying-on of hands and for deficiency of intention in the English Ordinal. But though it was convulsed with internecine strife, the English Nation was solid in regarding the Papacy as an alien power and, even when it reached them, Englishmen in the seventeenth century, except the minute few, had no ears for papalist propaganda.

Whatever else worried the Non-jurors in the eighteenth century, they did not worry themselves about the validity of Anglican Orders; nor, for that matter, did anybody else until the middle of the nineteenth century.

That the Tractarian Movement, reasserting as it did the Catholic aspect of the Anglican tradition, would in any case have invited a papalist attack on Anglican Orders, is obvious. But the theology of the validity of Orders would have remained caviare to the general, and the question of the validity of Anglican Orders of interest only to the theologian, if it had not been for the quasi-congregationalism which, as the Tractarian Movement developed into what is known as the Anglo-Catholic Revival, became a feature of the Church of England.

Many circumstances conspired to produce that quasi-congregationalism. The old concept of the identity of the nation and the Church was becoming an anachronism. What we now call the Free Churches had evolved into recognised and powerful institutions. A man's religion was coming to be considered as much a part of his proper predilection as the cut of his clothes. The long period of peace and natural progress and intellectual ferment which followed the Napoleonic wars had set in. The Tractarians' reassertion of the Catholic aspect of the Anglican tradition had found expression, not only in the teaching of parish clergy, but in the services of parish churches. Attempts to suppress the ritual movement by legal prosecution failed; and that movement provoked a counter emphasis of the Protestant aspect of the Anglican tradition which also found its expression in the teaching of parish clergy and in the services of parish churches.

As the decades passed, the contrasts of the extremes became more sharp, until, by the beginning of the twentieth century, all over the country, and often side by side, were to be found parishes in which on the one hand the Mass was rendered with every ritual accompaniment and the teaching and practice were in accordance, and on the other hand Evening Communion was given prominence and the teaching and practice were in accordance. To the foreign or superficial observer the effect seemed to be that the Church of England was divided into two churches, which were held together only by the establishment. That, of course, was not the case. While the teaching given, and the services of the parish churches, varied more or less one from another, they graded as it were in either direction from a central type of which the cathedrals provided the norm; and the great mass of English Church folk remained simply Church folk, and so long as extreme practices were not forced upon them, they did not trouble their heads.

None the less, though those seriously affected by it have always been relatively few, the quasi-congregationalism which began to obtain in the Church of England in the fifties produced among many Anglo-Catholics a disproportionate sensitiveness in regard to the validity of Anglican Orders. When a man whose way of religious life was to join in offering the Eucharistic Sacrifice on a Sunday, and who before his Communion resorted to Confession, was told, "Your Mass is no Mass at all and your Absolution is no Absolution; for your priest is no priest", the argument became *ad hominem.* It was not only the Roman Catholic propagandist—and happily the English Roman Catholic had begun to be recognized as being as true an Englishman as any other—who told him so. It was his fellow English Churchman in the next parish, who, however unconsciously, forced him to ask whether he had any real sacramental life at all. And further, as time went on, the growing quasi-congregationalism of the Church of England was accompanied for Anglo-Catholics by an ever-increasing consciousness of schism from the rest of historic Christendom. The reunion of the Anglican Communion with the Latin West not being on the horizon, their eyes turned to the Orthodox East, to which throughout its revolt from Rome it had made a persistent appeal. But when from the forties onwards such men as William Palmer or H. P. Liddon visited Moscow or Constantinople, they were met by a shake of the head and told, "We know nothing about you except that you are a Protestant and Reformed"; while at the Bonn Conferences in the seventies, despite von Döllinger, the Dutch Old Catholics joined the Russians in saying much the same. It was thus that, with their whole position fiercely scouted from within by the extreme Protestant Anglicans, and attacked from without by the Roman controversialists, with the central Anglicans at least doubtful whither their faces were set, cold-shouldered by the Orthodox and rebuffed even by the Dutch Old Catholics, all that Anglo-Catholics could do was to hold fast and, carrying on their sacramental life as best they might, wait for better days. That in such isolation the validity of Anglican Orders must have been a matter of personal concern to many Anglo-Catholics goes without saying, but I venture to doubt whether their successors of to-day can realize how Anglo-Catholics in the nineties were troubled thereby.

Imponderabilia are generally more important than *ponderabilia.* It was not that the case for Anglican Orders was weak or badly stated. On the contrary, as is apparent if, say, T. A. Lacey's statement of it in the nineties be compared with that of Dom Gregory Dix last year, their defence has become increasingly convincing. Men such as Lord Halifax, who longed and laboured for reunion with Rome, were as unshaken by the attack on Anglican Orders as were Charles Gore and other anti-Papalists. Whereas, if the case against their validity had been strong, Anglo-Catholic converts to Rome would have been numbered in shoals, relatively they were few and far between, and rarely of intellectual or other distinction.

But to form a reasoned judgment on so technical a question as the validity of Orders predicated theological and historical equipment. In the stress of their difficult position, and in their isolation, the mere facts of the Roman Catholic attack on Anglican Orders, and their non-recognition by the Orthodox, produced among Anglo-Catholics, if not uneasiness, at least a certain restlessness and impatient desire tc get their validity vindicated.

It was the existence of that desire which produced Fr. Brandreth's *episcopi vagantes*, who, for all their nuisance value, cannot be regarded as other than a by-product of a phase of the Anglo-Catholic revival.

The conditions which called them into being were, on the one hand, that it was currently received as dogma that, no matter how or by whom an *episcopus vagans* had been consecrated, so long as his consecration satisfied the exoteric test of "matter, form and minister" and the esoteric test of "intention", he was endowed with power to confer 'valid' Orders on any man on whom he chose to confer them; and, on the other hand, although only a small minority of Anglo-Catholics were unsettled by the arguments advanced against the validity of their Orders, Anglo-Catholics as a whole were disturbed and embarrassed by the doubts which were in the air as to whether their priests were true priests, their Mass a true Mass, their absolutions, true absolutions, and so on.

Whatever my personal estimate may be worth, it is that the climax of opportunity for the *episcopus vagans* was reached in the nineties, and that since the Papal condemnation of Anglican Orders in 1896 that opportunity has progressively diminished. If those who had hoped confidently for a *rapprochement* with Rome were chilled and discouraged by that condemnation, the general body of Anglo-Catholics was surprised by the weakness of the case against Anglican Orders as set out in the Papal Bull, and in themselves received it paradoxically as in fact a verdict for their defence. As I see things, if my dear friend l'Abbé Portal had not forced the issue, and Lord Halifax and T. A. Lacey had not gone to the Vatican, the opportunity for *episcopi vagantes* as, so to speak, camp followers, hovering on the flanks of the Anglo-Catholic Communion, would have been vastly greater and more serious.

The future is always unpredictable, but, writing to-day, I should forecast that twenty years hence only traces of those of whom Fr. Brandreth writes will remain, and that they will be little more than a souvenir, as of a disease.

A glance at Fr. Brandreth's pages will confirm and illustrate what I have written above as to the demand for 'valid' Orders and as to the ability to supply them being, in effect, the sole *raison d'être* of our contemporary *episcopi vagantes*.

The story begins with Dr. Lee and his mysterious Order of Corporate Reunion, as to which nothing whatever appears to be now capable of verification, and in which, with many of my friends, I was curiously interested in the nineties. All that we, or, I think, anyone, knew was that Lee and his two fellow *episcopi vagantes* were said to have received valid and incontestable consecration, and conferred valid priestly ordination on Anglican clergy who joined their Order; as to its constitution, or even the number of its members, no one had the remotest notion. I myself never came across a member of it, and although a few years before his death it came about that I made Dr. Lee's acquaintance, and both liked and respected him for his obvious sincerity of life, he shrank into his shell whenever I tried to open the subject of his consecration or of the Order. My impression is that whatever may have been the secret past of the Order, it was then practically extinct; but the point which I desire to emphasise here is that the rumours current about Lee and his Order in the seventies and eighties would have fallen on deaf ears if he and it had not advanced the pretension of being instruments ready to hand for the provision of the Anglican Communion with a hierarchy, the Orders of which must be received as incontestable by all the historic Churches of Christendom. That he himself had no qualms as to the validity of the Anglican priesthood I am very sure, but I conceive it to be probable that at one time he thought the disruption of the Church of England to be certain, in which event he looked to being called to provide the Anglo-Catholic section of it with a valid ministry. In sum and substance I adjudge that he is to be exonerated as an example of the axiom that supply answers demand, or, in other words, that if a pathological case, he was sincere. In illustration of the interest which he aroused, I recall how in 1892, when I was one of a party of theological students which V. S. S.

Coles of the Pusey House was entertaining at Shepton Beauchamp, an American named Kinsman, who afterwards became a bishop of the Protestant Episcopal Church, startled us by announcing that as soon as he was ordained he purposed to seek conditional re-ordination from Lee, about whom he knew no more than we.

That Dr. Pusey himself should have thought it worth while to examine Ferrete's claim to have been consecrated by the Syrian Orthodox (Jacobite) Metran of Homs is abundant evidence that he judged the mischievous possibilities of that obscure *episcopus vagans* offering 'valid' Orders broadcast to Anglican clergy to be not inconsiderable. Those possibilities being nipped in the bud, Ferrete disappeared, but the traces which Fr. Brandreth records him to have left behind him show what he might otherwise have done.

As to whether Vernon Herford ever received episcopal consecration, I cannot but be doubtful. I came to know him with some closeness in the tens and twenties. He was a man of ample means and of simplicity of life, and was in every way kindly, devout, gentle and modest. Mar Timotheos, the Assyrian Metropolitan of Travancore, told him in my presence to his face in 1920 that he must have been tricked by an impostor, and again in 1925 the present Mar Shimun told him and two of the priests whom he had ordained that the Assyrians know nothing of his consecration. Whatever were the facts—and I could never get him to speak of them—I have no doubt but that essentially his was a case for a psychiatrist. Thirty years ago, though probably not numerous, the group of those who received priest's Orders at his hands was worthy of attention. Among others it included Dr. Orchard,[1] a theologian of ability, and a dynamic preacher who, being then the minister of a Congregationalist church in London—the King's Weigh House—with the agreement of his people, celebrated Mass in it every Sunday and gave Catholic teaching. It is much to be desired that someone who had part in it would write the story of the group while there is time.

That, however they began, the primal *episcopi vagantes* of our time ended by becoming little more than fountains of 'valid Orders' is above all exemplified by the cases of Arnold Harris Mathew and of Joseph René Vilatte, but for whom

[1] Before he became a convert to Rome, he discussed with Lord Davidson the possibility of members of the Group being received as a kind of extra-diocesan Order into the Church of England.

there would have been no great practical reason for Fr. Brandreth to have compiled this book. That Mathew, whose personal character was beyond reproach, was a restless and perhaps a turbulent man, all who knew him are agreed. His impetuous way was to conceive ambitious visions and, propounding them with magniloquence, to convince himself and others that they were realisable. The late Old Catholic Archbishop Kennick of Utrecht, who was the Principal of Amersfoort when his predecessor, Archbishop Gul, consecrated Mathew in 1908, described to me how Mathew simply hypnotised the Dutch Old Catholic hierarchy into believing that the Church of England was actually in process of breaking up, and that the great majority of Anglo-Catholics would be eager to unite under his leadership, and with them a large secession of English Roman Catholics. All that they were waiting for was his own consecration to be their bishop.

Mathew, no doubt, had also hynotized himself to the same effect, but his vision belonged to nephelococcygia. His English adherents never numbered more than a few hundred, and the English Old Catholic Church, of which he proclaimed himself the founder, never assumed reality. When they were disillusioned, the Dutch Old Catholic bishops declared, as Archbishop Rinkel told us at Edinburgh in 1937, that, Mathew having obtained his consecration by misrepresentation, they regarded his acts as null and void, and could not recognise as bishops those on whom he professed to have conferred episcopal Orders.

A study of the lines of *episcopi vagantes* which Fr. Brandreth has traced so industriously as originating in Mathew will show that none of them founded a homogeneous sect. In England their lay followings have been infinitesimal. Some few of them, indeed, have formed as it were eclectic congregations, but otherwise they have been more or less underground workers whose sole activity has been the conferring of 'valid' Orders on cryptic groups of Anglican clergy. In America, where the macédoine of religio-nationalities provided the opportunity, they have come more into the open, and have equipped with a valid ministry what in effect were derelict secessions from the historic communions of Europe, or strange and fortuitous congeries which had come together from racial and other causes.

Joseph René Vilatte and his career were in most things in sharp contrast to Mathew and his career. His theatre was U.S.A. He was not an Anglo-Saxon. He was a convert with a chequered past to Anglicanism from Rome. His activities were to a great extent among Belgians and other immigrants to U.S.A. But, like Mathew's, first and last his importance depended entirely on his being an *episcopus vagans* who conferred 'valid' Orders. Indeed, unlike Mathew, he made no pretence of having received consecration to be bishop of an existing Church. His dubious consecrator, Alvares, was himself something like an *episcopus vagans*, and the story of his consecration is fantastic to a degree. When, in view of the forthcoming Lambeth Conference of 1930, I inquired of the Syrian-Orthodox Patriarch of Antioch, Mar Elias, and of the Metran of Homs, Mar Severus Barsawm, who is now the Patriarch Mar Ephrem, both described him as a "liar and a cheat" and declared that he was no bishop.

Having, like Mathew, failed to form a Church, he ended, like him, in being unashamedly an *episcopus vagans* who was a fountain of 'valid' Orders. Fr. Brandreth, who has been indefatigable in tracing the ramifications of the Vilatte 'succession', rightly points out that Frederick Ebenezer John Lloyd, whom Vilatte consecrated with right of succession to himself in 1915, was largely responsible for their complexity and relative importance. Vilatte seems to have lost heart at his initial failure to form a new Church and to have become inert. Lloyd, who was forceful, clever, ambitious and—he married a Peabody—possessed of ample means, set himself to found his cryptic 'Order of Antioch', which was open to any Anglican clergyman who received 'valid' Orders from him. At the same time he imparted 'valid' Episcopal Orders to several Churches which came into being from different causes, but over which he claimed no jurisdiction. For example, when in 1921, at the height of the negro revolt against the colour bar, the "African Orthodox Church" was formed in U.S.A., Lloyd consecrated bishops for it, which bishops in their turn consecrated bishops for a branch of it which later came into being in South Africa, and the *American Year Book of Churches* for 1945 lists no fewer than five 'churches' of contrasted type and varying origin, which are recognisable as being within the Vilatte ambit by their prominent and mysterious boast that they possess 'the Antiochene Episcopal Succession'. In this way Lloyd succeeded in creating a loose organisation in which he was looked to as the central *episcopus vagans*, and which consisted partly of such churches, but still more of an underground clientèle of Anglican clergymen who belonged also to his

B

Order of Antioch and owed him allegiance. Moreover, having reached in 1925 a concordat with several of the *episcopi vagantes* who derived from Mathew, he found means to extend that Order to England, where, incredible though it may appear, ten years ago it had begun to attract an appreciable, if not large, membership, which was diffused all over England, and included a number of Anglican clergy.

Churchill Sibley, Lloyd's 'Vicar-General' for Great Britain, who had previously been the organist at a South London church, was an able and charming man, and worked tactfully, successfully, and withal with effective subreption, to spread the Order. I myself had been aware that something of the kind was going on, but in 1934 I was startled when, on entering the sacristry of the Armenian Church of St. Sarkis, Iverna Gardens, Kensington, I found Sibley there vested in surplice and stole, and was told by him that though he had been an Anglican, he was no longer so exclusively, but that he belonged to an Order which was truly Catholic, and was a priest of the Antiochene succession. On inquiry of my very dear but simple friend, the Armenian priest of London, Father Khosrov, I discovered that Sibley had approached him a couple of years before and, showing him a copy of the so-called Bull of Vilatte's consecration by the Syrian-Orthodox Patriarch Peter of Antioch, which is the charter of the Vilatte succession, had urged that since the Syrian-Orthodox Church and the Armenian Church are in full communion, by the right of hospitality the use of St. Sarkis should be accorded to himself and to Lloyd's Order of Antioch. Taking that document at its face value, Father Khosrov had welcomed Sibley and given him the use of St. Sarkis for gatherings of the Order of Antioch. When I told him that the authorities of the Syrian-Orthodox Church had repudiated the Vilatte succession, he at once referred the matter to the Armenian Patriarch at Jerusalem, who in due course instructed him to cease all relations with Sibley and the Order. But meanwhile, Lloyd himself having visited England to initiate a forward drive of the Order, I received a further unpleasant eye-opener as to its cryptic pervasiveness. For, being shown by Father Khosrov a photograph of a group taken at St. Sarkis after Lloyd had held an ordination of priests, deacons and deaconesses, I saw in it the fairly well-known incumbents of two London parishes and a member of an Anglican sisterhood, whose names nothing would induce me to print. A glance at

Fr. Brandreth's Vilatte List No. 5 will show that shortly afterwards Lloyd consecrated Sibley as his Archbishop of England and Vicar-General of the Order. As to the success of the drive upon which Sibley engaged, I had no means of judging. But the fact that Lloyd, who had become head of the Intercollegiate University which is not recognized as Kappa-beta-phi by Harvard, Yale, Columbia, etc., but the degrees of which, since it has a State charter, are printed in Crockford, proceeded also through Sibley to scatter honorary doctorates on English clergymen, shows its vigour and perhaps betrays its method. That its impulse has died out is probable, but its vestiges remain.

Fr. Brandreth has dealt in this book very fully with the question as to whether or not, on being received into the Anglican Communion, men who have received putative Orders from Mathew and Vilatte should be re-ordained. That question, which, of course, is of real importance, is a principal reason why we begged him to compile this book, in order that the facts might be easily available for the next Lambeth Conference. But as I see things, a question of even greater importance is the attitude of the Anglican Episcopate, and especially of our English bishops, towards those of the Anglican clergy who have received, or may receive, such Orders at the hands of *episcopi vagantes*. As the law stands, it is probably the case that English diocesans have no power to do more than censure an incumbent who receives such Orders, and it is noteworthy that as was undoubtedly the case with the two clergymen to whom I have referred above, there are, however mistakenly, those among them who, in receiving these Orders, have been actuated by the highest motives. On the other hand, that Anglican clergymen, being bound together in a cryptic Order of which the head is an *episcopus vagans*, would have, as it were, a double church life and their allegiance be divided between him and their canonical diocesan, to phrase it gently, would appear to be preposterous.

CHAPTER I

INTRODUCTION

In his study of *Episcopi Vagantes in Church History* Dr. A. J. Macdonald has traced the historic *episcopus vagans* of the Middle Ages to a number of causes. The primary cause of wandering, at least in the East, appears to have been the deprivation of office, though not of episcopal status, on account of heresy or misconduct. The method of popular election, by which a bishop might be consecrated to a See which subsequently refused to elect him, also compelled a number of prelates to wander in order to seek a livelihood. In the West, and less frequently in the East, the *chorepiscopi* were a cause of trouble, while at a later period in the West the wandering missionary bishops from Ireland perambulated the Continent in large numbers.

Dr. Macdonald has shown how again and again councils and synods legislated against the *vagantes*, less because their episcopal status was doubtful than because their wandering habits disrupted the course of diocesan administration. It was only at a later period that the episcopal status of certain of the *vagabundi* became open to question, and that mainly in the case of the Irish bishops.

The modern *episcopus vagans* is less easy to classify than his historic predecessor, and the grounds of objection against him are different. In some respects the title is misleading, since the majority of these prelates do not wander as their predecessors did. On the other hand, the majority of them combine the disadvantages of the historic *episcopi vagantes* of both the earlier and later periods; they invade jurisdiction, and in most cases their episcopal status is doubtful. To-day a man is placed in this category who has, or claims to have, received irregular or clandestine consecration; or, having been consecrated regularly and canonically, has been excommunicated by, or otherwise cut off from, the Church which consecrated him, and is not in communion with any historic metropolitical See. The main ground of objection against him is that, in spite of resounding claims to the contrary, his episcopal status is doubtful, and that, even if his orders be valid, the exercise of them is not legitimate.

In many cases the church over which he claims to preside appears to exist, if it exists at all except on paper, for the sake of the bishop rather than the bishop for the sake of the Church.

The modern *episcopus vagans* presents various problems to those charged with ecclesiastical administration. At the present time there are considerably more than a hundred and twenty such bishops living, of whom more than thirty are resident in Great Britain, and the total number is greatly increased if one adds the number of exotic sects in America which claim to possess bishops, but do not claim a succession, and the number of African natives who claim the title 'bishop' merely in order to gain prestige in the eyes of their tribe.

The *episcopi vagantes* of the present day are grouped into four main streams of succession, although others periodically arise, and after a brief time depart for the obscurity whence they came. These various streams of succession each present peculiar features and problems of their own, and not only this, but their representatives are men who differ widely from each other: some are honest and believe that they have a genuine vocation to guide, in isolation from the rest of Christendom, the small handful of people which acknowledges their claims; others are clearly not honest, and use their supposed episcopal status as a means of personal enrichment at the expense of any who are so misguided as to support them; others, again, are mentally unbalanced.

These differences make it impossible to lay down any clearly defined psychology of episcopal vagrancy, or to enunciate any general rules of psychological causation. In a very large number of them, however, one can discern something of that state known as 'fantasy', which, in the words of Dr. Rudolf Allers, "provides an imaginary world for the day-dreamer, in which all those factors which trouble him in the world of reality, are either eliminated or converted into their opposites."[1] It is, indeed, a method of compensation which seeks to balance a subjectively experienced inferiority. But, to quote Dr. Allers again, "as this imaginary world exists only at the pleasure of the dreamer and the events of that world are what he chooses to make them, he is in truth the creator, protector and law-giver of that world. Man's helplessness and impotence are trans-

[1] *Psychology of Character*, ed. of 1939, p. 87. Probably this would not apply to those who conceive a vocation to their position.

formed into unlimited power; the restrictions to creative achievement give way to actual omnipotence."[1] All this may be conditioned by religious feelings, ideas, emotions and ideals, and it would seem to be along some such line as this that the psychological problems presented by the bulk of the modern *episcopi vagantes* may best be approached. The condition of fantasy is common enough, but certain religious interests or instincts have, in these cases, given to it this strange form.

The kind of thing which may happen is this: John Smith comes into contact with an *episcopus vagans*. He has certain social ambitions, and he has seen the social standing of the clergy. He therefore flatters the bishop, tells him that he wants to give his life to the service of God, and begins to serve the bishop's Mass. As soon as he has become efficient at the altar the bishop makes him a deacon, and then, when he has learned to say Mass, ordains him priest. John Smith has been made a priest solely on the merits of being able to say Mass with reasonable efficiency; he is uneducated, and his lack of cultural equipment may even be such that he finds difficulty in composing ordinary correspondence. Having been made a priest, he begins to work more on the bishop. He starts by telling him that, as he is head of an independent church, he ought to be an archbishop. But an archbishop must have suffragans, jurisdiction over whom justifies the claim to archiepiscopal status. John Smith and one of his fellow-priests are therefore "elected" by a synod of sycophants and consecrated. After the consecration the consecrator is elected archbishop. Thus matters continue for a few weeks until John Smith quarrels with his superior and proclaims himself independent. Whether he does that or not, the point is that the consecrator had some smattering at least of education, and knew matter, form and intention. John Smith's mind is a blank on such premises, though he may be able to chatter a jargon and deceive people as to his knowledge.

The ecclesiastical problems presented by this sort of proceeding admit of no easy solution, and while all the *episcopi vagantes* are not of the kind of John Smith and his consecrator, yet a considerable number of them are, so that it is not always possible even to decide upon the technical validity of their orders according to Western theories of transmission. The problems presented by some of these bishops will emerge more fully as we examine each stream of

[1] *Psychology of Character*, ed. of 1939, p. 87.

succession. Certain principles, however, may be enunciated now.

The Lambeth Conference of 1920, in dealing with the case of Bishop Mathew, laid down the following: "The circumstances of Bishop Mathew's consecration are so uncertain, and his subsequent isolation is so complete, that, without casting any sort of reflection on the validity of Old Catholic Orders, or discussing the theological question of abstract 'validity', we feel that as a matter of practice, in the event of persons ordained by him or by his successors desiring to come over to the Anglican Church, and exercise their ministry in communion with it, the only proper course would be for them (if in all respects suitable) to be ordained *sub conditione*."[1] This paragraph is not entirely satisfactory. There was really no uncertainty about Mathew's actual consecration at all, and there can be no doubt that his own Orders were valid, though there is grave doubt as to the worth of the acts of some of those in succession from him. The point which appears to have been in the minds of the bishops, however, was that these *episcopi vagantes* could not be regarded as having any Church behind them. The point which governed their decision, in their own words, was that "on a review of all the facts they are driven to the conclusion that it is not possible to regard the so-called 'Old Catholic Church in Great Britain' . . . as a properly constituted branch of the Church." [2] This objection applies to all the bodies presided over by the *episcopi vagantes*. Even the perfectly orthodox, respectable and self-contained Rite presided over by Mgr. Bernard M. Williams, Bishop Mathew's successor,[3] is not in communion with any historic See, and is, in fact, repudiated by the Western Patriarchate, of which it claims to be a part.

The fact that all these organisations are repudiated by the Churches from which they originally obtained their Orders adds to the difficulty of dealing with them, especially in the case of those deriving from Eastern Churches, which hold the doctrine that Holy Orders are defectible through heresy or schism. While the Church of England is not necessarily bound by the repudiations issued by other Churches, she is, on the other hand, often in friendly contact with those Churches, and may in most cases rightly presume that the successions have not been lightly or wantonly abandoned. In view of these facts, it seems undesirable for the Church of England to accord any recognition to the

[1] *Report*, p. 155. [2] *Ibid.* [3] See pp. 16 and 19.

various rites and organisations represented by the *episcopi vagantes*, but her attitude towards the individual bishops would preferably take account of the particular circumstances in each case; if an individual bishop or priest of one of these successions were a man of upright life, genuinely convinced of the rightness of his position, anomalous though it must be by Anglican standards, it would clearly be wrong for the Anglican Church to place herself in the position of a persecutor.

A fundamental difficulty with regard to the claims of many of these organisations, both in England and America, is that no valid reason appears to be forthcoming for the attempts to found Eastern rites for Western Christians. The historic Eastern Churches, strongly as they repudiate Papal claims to domination, regard the Pope as Patriarch of the West, and have never at any time obtruded themselves within what they regard as his patriarchal jurisdiction, beyond making lawful provision for the spiritual needs of their own people. All these successions are repudiated by Archbishop Germanos, representative in England of the Œcumenical Patriarch.

It is an unhappy fact that certain of these bishops trade on the fact that the average Anglican clergyman knows nothing about them and is, perhaps, even unaware of the streams of succession which they represent. From time to time, therefore, they appear in various parishes claiming to be genuine Eastern or Old Catholic prelates, and are accorded the honour due to their supposed position. It may therefore be stated at once that there is no Old Catholic bishop resident in England who is recognised as such either by the See of Utrecht or by the Church of England, and that the only recognised body of Old Catholics in America is the Polish National Catholic Church, under Bishop Hodur of Scranton. Furthermore, if a prelate claims to be a bishop of the Church of Antioch, it is well to verify his claim before permitting him to perform any ecclesiastical function. Neglect of such simple precautions may result in scandals which do much harm to the cause of true religion.

CHAPTER II

VALIDITY AND REGULARITY

In dealing with *episcopi vagantes* one is faced with their claim to possess valid Orders, and in some instances they are able to produce evidence to support succession from some undisputed source. It is necessary, therefore, to give some consideration to the subject of validity.

Broadly speaking, the Catholic Church knows two theories of validity, which may be termed the Augustinian and the non-Augustinian. The Augustinian theory is generally accepted in the West, but has never received acceptance in the East. According to this theory a bishop who has been validly consecrated does, when excommunicated or otherwise cut off from the Church, retain the power of transmitting a succession of valid, if irregular, Orders. The Augustinian would not only say, "Once a bishop, always a bishop", but he would go on to say, "Once possessing the powers of a bishop, always possessing the powers of a bishop".[1] The Augustinian is compelled, therefore, to go on to distinguish between the power conferred in ordination and consecration, and the legitimate exercise of that power. "Heretics have the power to pass it on," says Tixeront, "but they do not possess and cannot pass on its legitimate exercise."[2] Having discussed various other views of the matter, the same authority goes on to say: "The Church and sound theology have rejected all these systems and vain explanations. Distinguishing the validity from the legitimacy or permissibility of ordination, they insist that

[1] The *locus classicus* is St. Augustine, *Contra Epistolam Parmeniani*, II, 28: "Multis modis apparet frustra et inaniter dici. Primo, quia nulla ostenditur causa cur ille qui ipsum baptismum amittere non potest, ius dandi potest amittere. Utrumque enim sacramentum est; et quadam consecratione utrumque homini datur: illud, cum baptizatur; istud, cur ordinatur: ideoque in Catholica utrumque non licet iterari. Nam si quando ex ipsa parte venientes etiam præposito, pro bono pacis, correcto schismatis errore suscepti sunt, et si visum est opus esse ut eadem officia gererent quæ gerebant, non sunt rursus ordinati; sed sicut baptismus in eis, ita ordinatio mansit integra: quia in præcisione fuerat vitium, quod unitatis pace correctum est, non in sacramentis quæ ubicumque sunt ipsa sunt."

[2] *L'Ordre et les Ordinations*, 2nd ed., p. 202.

ordination is always valid when a true bishop, whoever he may be, performs the essential rites upon the ordinand; but that, for this ordination to be legitimate it is necessary that both the bishop and the ordinand should be in a state determined by law."[1]

The non-Augustinian view is quite different from this. For the non-Augustinian, Orders are valid only within the context of the Mystical Body of Christ. This is certainly the view of St. Cyprian,[2] for whom the idea of validity is inseparable from that of legitimacy. The view of the Eastern Church generally is Cyprianic or non-Augustinian. The general Orthodox position is most clearly put forward in the following statement:[3]

"(a) The Orthodox hold themselves unable to pronounce an opinion on the 'validity of Orders' given outside the Communion of the Orthodox Church, i.e. in the sense of whether or not the *charisma*—the scholastic precisions of 'Character', etc., are foreign to Orthodoxy—of episcopal and other Orders is at all conferred by heterodox episcopal consecrations or by heterodox ordinations of priests and deacons. To them all schisms—the Roman Catholic Church as well as the Anglican, Old Catholic and the Monophysite Churches or the Protestant non-episcopal Reformed Churches —are schisms not *within* the One Holy Catholic and Apostolic Church but *from* the One Holy Catholic Church which they identify in limitation to their own Communion. In effect they do not deny categorically that other Churches *may* be part of the One Holy Catholic Apostolic Church. All that they state dogmatically is that unless and until full dogmatic agreement be duly affirmed between themselves and those Churches, they cannot recognise them as integral to *the* Church. And in consequence, even if all the exoteric marks of 'validity' be recognisable in the succession of the episcopate of those Churches and in their ministration of Holy Orders, and even if the dogmatic tradition of those Churches in regard to the exoteric significance of episcopal

[1] *L'Ordre et les Ordinations*, 2nd ed., p. 211. See Saltet, *Les Réordinations*, for a full discussion of the whole subject from the Augustinian side.

[2] e.g. *Ep.* lxix, 5: "'Unus grex et unus pastor.' Si autem grex unus est, quomodo potest gregi adnumerari qui in numero gregis non est? aut pastor habere quomodo potest qui, manente vero pastore et in ecclesia Dei ordinatione succedanea præsidente, nemini succedens et a se ipse incipiens alienus fit et profanus."

[3] From a private Memorandum by Canon J. A. Douglas entitled *The Significance of Interconsecration between two Churches from the General Eastern Standpoint.*

consecrations, or of the ordering of priests and deacons, be consistent, or identical, with their own, they hold themselves free to accept those who have received them as bishops, priests and deacons, and as at their discretion, i.e. to be free to receive them as such or to reiterate their ordination or consecration. . . .

(b) The apparent inconsistency, as Western theologians may *prima facie* judge the action of the Orthodox, is explained by the principle of Economy, sc. the principle that the Church being *tamiouchos*, i.e. holding the duty of stewardship in her own household (so long as she does not transgress her dogmatic tradition as revealed by Christ through His Apostles in Holy Scripture, as precised by the Œcumenical Councils and as preserved in the writings of the Fathers and by the *paradosis* of the Holy Spirit through the centuries) is free and indeed is bound to exercise her stewardship by accepting or rejecting heterodox sacramental ministrations accordingly as she judges her doing so to be for the advancement of the Kingdom of Christ and the good of human souls, or the reverse. . . .

"(e) In other words, while exoteric requirements, which for the present purpose may be categorised as the proper matter, form and minister, and the esoteric significance of 'intention' are as necessary for the acceptance of a consecration or an ordination from the Orthodox viewpoint as, e.g. from the Roman Catholic viewpoint, *the additional, preliminary, and indeed supreme requirement for the acceptance of a consecration or an ordination is their authenticity, sc. that the bishops who performed the consecration, or the bishop who performed the ordination, had authority to perform it. . . .*[1]

"(f) In this respect I should point out that, as in the case of other Greek theological terms which are translated by Latin theological terms, e.g. *propitiatory* and *exilastikos*, much confusion arises from the use of the term 'validity' as equivalent in contents to the term '*kuriotes*'.

"Whatever contents be ascribed to the term 'validity' of Orders, its etymological stress directs the mind to the question as to whether or not the bishop consecrated or the priest ordained, be a true bishop or priest in the sense that he has received *charisma* having received which he has power to perform the sacramental ministration of a bishop or a priest. And it is thus that for many Anglican theologians as well as for all Roman Catholic theologians, it is a

[1] Italics as in original.

dogmatic presumption that a single *episcopus vagans*, no matter what his heresy, how or from whom he received his Orders, so long as his consecration satisfies the exoteric requirements of 'matter, form and minister' and the esoteric requirement of 'intention', must be regarded as being possessed indefectibly of all the powers of the episcopate, and on being received into the communion of the Church, cannot be reconsecrated without profanation, but must be received in his Orders; and that the same holds in regard to priests and deacons ordained by him.

"On the other hand, the Orthodox term '*kuriotetes*' tends to sidetrack the above line of thought and to confine the issue to the question as to whether or not a bishop or priest was consecrated or ordained by lawful authority. If he was, his Orders are *enkuros*. If he was not, his Orders are *akuros*—and there is no profit in further investigating them unless he accedes to Orthodoxy. . . .

"(h) The theologies of Monophysite Christendom, sc. the Coptic, Syrian-Orthodox (Jacobite) and the Armenian Churches await detailed comparative examination and scientific presentation. And their materials are limited and hard of access. But as I understand the matter, the Coptic, Syrian-Orthodox and Armenian dogmatic traditions are identical with what I have outlined above as that of the Greek Orthodox Communion; and their practice is wholly consistent with the premise that for the acceptance of heterodox Orders the one and supreme consideration is authenticity."

The Church of England is not officially bound to either of these theories, though in practice she inclines to the Augustinian.[1] Bishop John Wordsworth of Salisbury, probably the greatest Anglican authority on the subject, was quite clear that the Church of England was Augustinian. "Using the word 'Sacrament' in the broader sense given to it by ancient theology, which, of course, includes under the term other efficacious signs of sacred realities than those of the two great Sacraments of the Gospel, we hold in the Church of England, quite as strongly, I think, as is held in any part of Christendom, that the 'Sacrament of Order' requires laying-on of hands, with prayer suitable to the office conferred, and with a general intention of making

[1] As, for example, the Lambeth Conference in the conditions required before permitting intercommunion with the Scandinavian Churches.

a man what the Church intends as Bishop, Priest, or Deacon. We hold that such an Ordination conferred by a Bishop, as sole or chief minister, who has been himself so ordained, even if he is a heretic, is valid and cannot be reiterated without sacrilege, and that it is impossible to bind the power so conferred by Church censure."[1] That sums up the general consensus of the opinion of Anglican divines on the subject, though it may be noted that such an interpretation is not demanded either by the Preface to the Ordinal or by those of the Articles of Religion which treat of the matter of ordination.[2]

Neither of these theories is wholly satisfactory. The non-Augustinian, if carried to its logical conclusion, would mean either that valid Orders do not exist at all, or would limit the possession of them to one part only of the Catholic Church. The Augustinian theory, on the other hand, if strictly construed, tends to divorce the power of Orders from the stream of the Church's life.[3] Clearly the sanction of the Church is necessary for the regular exercise of the power of Orders, and the writer of a recent article seems to have stated an important truth when he says that "regularity *where it may be had* is surely necessary to validity".[4] We should be inclined, therefore, to say that Orders which are wantonly irregular are, in fact, invalid and worthless. Any other conception must in the end lend countenance to an anarchy which is opposed to the very essence of the ordered life of the Body of Christ. Consecrations or ordinations which are performed for the sake of the persons being consecrated or ordained, rather than for the sake of the Church, are, at best, to use the phrase of Tertullian, "temerariae, leves, inconstantes".[5] They cannot be presumed valid.

The question arises, therefore, as to the most fruitful line of action to be adopted towards *episcopi vagantes*, or clerics ordained by them, who may wish to enter the Church of England. Any hard-and-fast rule is bound to appear arbitrary in view of the diversity of circumstances which have brought the successions into being and the differences

[1] *Ordination Problems*, pp. 10-11.

[2] The operative Articles are nos. XXIII, XXVI and XXXVI.

[3] " (The principle) of the objective efficacy of the sacraments has the preponderating influence; the subordination of the minister to the Church is maintained in as reduced a measure as possible." Saltet, *op. cit.*, p. 4.

[4] " Unitas Episcoporum " by H. Bryant Salmon in *Theology*, August 1944.

[5] *De Praescriptionibus Haereticorum*, 41.

in quality between the men concerned. The practice of the Roman Catholic Church, for apostates from her own faith who receive ordination or consecration from a heretical or schismatic bishop, is that on their return to the Church they are never allowed to exercise their Orders, and are, in fact, treated as though they had never received them. They are not, for example, bound to the recitation of the Office, or even to celibacy. "Ecclesiam non habere neque unquam habituram esse oratorem tamquam ordinatum, eumque propterea nullis teneri obligationibus statui clericalis annexis."[1] But by thus treating them as if they did not possess Orders, the Holy Office did not mean to imply that the ordination was therefore pronounced invalid; it simply refused to debate the matter. On the other hand, in the case of Dr. W. E. Orchard, who had been ordained by Vernon Herford[2] and who had never been a Roman Catholic, they gave conditional ordination.

Dr. John Wordsworth, holding firmly the Augustinian view of succession and speaking of "certain small schisms in England and America", is opposed to any form of re-ordination. "The facts of deposition or degradation, or of heresy in the ordaining bishop, must in such cases be set aside. Clergy validly ordained by a degraded or heretical bishop cannot be reordained. Whether they should be readmitted on penitence and licensed to officiate is quite another question, and of course the presence of the four conditions of a valid ordination must be ascertained."[3]

The present writer has had some experience in dealing with the *episcopi vagantes* and is strongly of the opinion that as a *rule* the Anglican Church should refuse to give them, or the clergy ordained by them, licence to minister within her communion but should require them, if they came to her, to give a solemn undertaking never to exercise their Orders and to retire into lay life. It would be necessary to impose the severest ecclesiastical penalties upon any person infringing such a condition. While this should be the rule, a power of dispensation from it in exceptional cases where the bishop or priest concerned appeared to have a true vocation to the Anglican ministry, might be vested in the Archbishop of Canterbury.

[1] Decree of the Holy Office dated November 18th, 1931. Cf. Gasparri, *Tractatus Canonicus de Matrimonio*, ed. of 1932, p. 371.

[2] See pp. 53ff.

[3] *Op. cit.*, p. 30.

CHAPTER III

THE MATHEW SUCCESSION

ARNOLD HARRIS MATHEW, the child of a mixed marriage, was originally prepared for the Anglican ministry, but was, in 1878, ordained priest in the Roman Catholic Church. After some years as a Roman Catholic parish priest in various places, a set of unfortunate circumstances for which he was not responsible caused him to leave the Roman Church; later he married. For a short period he acted as an Anglican curate at Holy Trinity Church, Sloane Street, with the sanction of the Bishop of London, Dr. Frederick Temple. Unfortunately the incumbent under whom he worked, the Rev. Robert Eyton, was a man of gravely immoral life, who shortly afterwards had to leave England to avoid exposure and disgrace. Mathew resigned, went to live in retirement in the country, wore lay dress and performed no ministerial functions. In 1907 he approached the Archbishop of Canterbury, Dr. Randall Davidson, with the proposal that he should be assigned some ministerial charge in the Church of England, but after some correspondence the project was abandoned.

In December, 1907, Mathew was approached by an ex-Roman priest called Richard O'Halloran, who informed him that there were 250 priests and congregations who wished for the ministrations of an Old Catholic bishop and that Mathew had been elected to that office by them. Negotiations were opened with the See of Utrecht, and Mathew wrote informing the Archbishop of Canterbury of what was going forward. On April 28th, 1908, he was consecrated bishop in St. Gertrude's Cathedral at Utrecht, by Archbishop Gul, assisted by the Old Catholic Bishops of Haarlem (J. J. van Thiel), Deventer (N. B. P. Spit) and Germany (J. Demmel).

Bishop Mathew returned to England immediately after his consecration, and appears at once to have discovered that the information given him by O'Halloran was entirely false and that the actual number of those willing to accept his ministrations was negligible. There seems to be no doubt that Mathew immediately informed Utrecht of the true state of affairs and added a request that he might be permitted to retire. The Dutch bishops exonerated him from personal blame in the following letter:

"We, the Archbishop and Bishops of the Old Catholic Church of Holland, and the Old Catholic Bishops of Germany and Switzerland, having heard with much concern of certain events connected with the English branch of the Old Catholic Church, wish to say that we have been in correspondence with a suspended Roman Catholic priest in England since the year 1902.

"This priest visited the Bishops of Bonn, Berne, Haarlem, Deventer, and the Archbishop of Utrecht, and we believed him to be in perfect accord with us. He accompanied Bishop Mathew on his visit to the Archbishop of Utrecht. On April 7th in the present year he, with others, signed the petition to the Bishops begging us to consecrate the Right Rev. A. H. Mathew.

"All the documents were sent by this priest to Bishop Herzog, accompanied by numerous letters urging upon us the immediate need of a Bishop, not only for the requirements of his own congregation, but for those of other clergy and congregations specified by him. We had no reason to suppose that we were mistaken in complying with his request. We wish now to state that our confidence in Bishop Mathew remains unshaken, after carefully perusing a large number of the documents bearing upon this matter, and we earnestly hope that his ministrations will be abundantly blessed by Almighty God, and that he will receive the cordial support of the British people and Church in the trying circumstances in which he has been placed.

"In the name of the Old Catholic Bishops of Holland, Germany and Switzerland,

The Secretary,

J. J. VAN THIEL, Bishop of Haarlem."[1]

There seems no reason to doubt the correctness of the view here taken by the Dutch bishops that the blame for the state of affairs attached to O'Halloran, and not to Mathew at this stage. For the two years following his consecration Mathew remained in full communion with Utrecht and with the status of a missionary bishop. In October, 1909, he was one of the assistants in Utrecht at the consecration of the Mariavite Bishop Jean Marie Kowalski by Archbishop Gul.

[1] *The Guardian*, June 3rd, 1908.

In September, 1909, Mathew attended the Old Catholic Congress at Vienna. At this Congress he claimed to have discovered various differences between the Old Catholics of Germany and Switzerland and the Church of the Netherlands, notably with regard to the acceptance of the decrees of the Synod of Jerusalem (1672),[1] the Sacrament of Penance, invocation of Saints, alterations in the Liturgy, and their general attitude to the Pope. No immediate step was taken, but in December, 1910, Mathew issued a 'Pastoral Letter' in which he declared his "autonomy and independence".[2] Differences had already occurred between Mathew and the Continental Old Catholics, and in August of that year Bishop van Thiel of Haarlem had written a letter[3] indicating that the Dutch Bishops recognised Mathew's movement as autonomous, but making it clear that, although in no way responsible for his acts and not seeing eye to eye with him, they were yet in full communion with one another.

In a formal pronouncement drawn up by the Old Catholic Bishops assembled at Utrecht in 1920 they state that Mathew's consecration was "surreptitiously secured by the production of false testimony, and would never have taken place had the consecrators known that the conditions stated in the questionable documents and required by our Episcopate were non-existent".[4] They also stated that upon the discovery of these facts they broke off intercourse with him. The present position of the Church of Utrecht in this matter is that the consecration was obtained *mala fide*, and that consequently it is null and void. They base this decision

[1] An English translation of these decrees was published in 1899 by J. N. W. B. Robertson, *The Acts and Decrees of the Synod of Jerusalem, sometimes called the Council of Bethlehem.*

[2] Printed in Mathew, *The Catholic Church of England*, pp. 20ff., and *An Episcopal Odyssey*, pp. 21ff.

[3] "Having seen in your issue of July 29th, Mr. Barber's letter on the Society of St. Willibrord, I wish to say that Mr. Barber is quite right in stating in his letter of last week that Bishop Mathew is in no sense a representative of the Church of Holland in England. Bishop Mathew is simply one of the Old Catholic Bishops, and, as such, he is in relation with the Old Catholics of Holland, and also, of course, with the Old Catholic Churches of Germany, Switzerland, and Austria, the Polish Catholic Church of America, and the Catholic Church of the Mariavites in Poland. In consequence of that, I wish to state that the Old Catholics in Holland and elsewhere could not be considered in any way responsible for Bishop Mathew's eventual particular attitude or opinions, because he only represents his own clergy and himself in England.

J. J. Van Thiel, Bishop of Haarlem."—*The Guardian*, August 5th, 1910.

[4] *Report of the Lambeth Conference*, 1920, p. 155.

on the ground that Mathew himself was responsible for the false testimony submitted in 1908 and, rather than being a victim of O'Halloran, was in fact his confederate. The 1920 Lambeth Conference, as we have seen above, (p. 4) did no more than express doubts as to the validity of the Mathew orders.

Bishop Mathew was personally devout, sincere and virtuous, with a genuine simplicity of character, but the story of his career from the time that he ceased to be in communion with Utrecht bears ample testimony to the fact that he was wholly unsuited for the position which he assumed as head of an independent religious organisation. Within twelve months of the break with Utrecht five bishops had been consecrated without any See or flock assigned to them. The story of these early consecrations is instructive for the light it throws upon Mathew's methods. Owing to the differences between himself and Utrecht, it was felt by his followers to be necessary to secure the episcopate to ensure that in the event of his death his movement should be able to continue, and his clergy no doubt pointed this out to him. Among his own clergy, who were in any case very few, he found no one suitable. He therefore decided to consecrate two men who had recently been deprived of the dignity of Monsignor by the Church of Rome. These two men were Herbert Ignatius Beale and Arthur William Howarth. Beale was already known to Mathew, and had retaliated against the deprivation by opening an 'Old Catholic' mission at Gunnersbury. Howarth was in trouble at this time with the Holy Office of the Inquisition owing to alleged irregularities with regard to Mass stipends. Both men seem to have been determined to recover the purple in the only way open to them—namely, by securing the episcopate by some means or other.[1] Mathew considered them to be men of sufficient age, wisdom and experience to secure the episcopate in trust for his Rite, and so consecrated them. Shortly after the consecration both men are said to have informed him that on no account would they exercise the episcopate, and that their sole object from then onwards would be to carry on their private quarrel with the Holy See.

[1] A somewhat different story is told by Howarth in a privately printed pamphlet, *A Protest against the Tyranny of the Roman Inquisition, &c.*, wherein he represents himself as never having considered receiving episcopal consecration until he received Mathew's offer, but little reliance can be placed upon this statement.

Mathew's clergy then proceeded to elect four of their number and to press for their consecration. Mathew acceded to their request, and consecrated Francis Bacon, Cuthbert Francis Hinton, Frederick Clement Christie Egerton and William Edmund Scott-Hall.[1] No reason seems to have been given as to why it was considered necessary to consecrate four men at once, but in the event all these prelates departed from the Rite after a short time.

The next person to be consecrated was Prince de Landas Berghes et de Rache, who soon afterwards went to America, where he was instrumental in founding two streams of succession to which we shall later refer. From Mathew's point of view the necessity of a bishop still remained, and in 1915 Willoughby was consecrated, only to be expelled when his true character became known. In April, 1916, Bernard Mary Williams was consecrated as Mathew's perpetual coadjutor with right of succession. At this time Mathew promised to consecrate no more bishops, but in spite of this he consecrated McFall later in the same year.

Mgr. Williams claims that he represents the only legitimate continuation of Mathew's Rite. This claim is justified, from his own point of view, by documentary evidence and the Rite over which he presides, extremely small though it is, stands on a higher level than the majority of the bodies dealt with in this book.

The most widespread of the Mathew lines of succession is that of the so-called Liberal Catholic Church. This body is a curious offshoot of the Theosophical Society, and its formation on its present lines appears to have been mainly due to a notorious colleague of Mrs. Annie Besant called Leadbeater.[2] The succession comes through Willoughby, and the whole movement was strongly condemned in its earlier stages by Mathew himself, who issued a *Pastoral Letter on Membership in the Theosophical Society and in the Order*

[1] For a further account of these bishops see the tables of succession on p. 22.

[2] Some account of Leadbeater will be found in *Round the World with a Dictaphone* by Sir Henry Lunn, ch. xv, together with other information concerning the Liberal Catholic Church. See also an article by W. Loftus Hare, 'The Crisis in the Theosophical Society' in *The Empire Review*, September, 1926. Stanley Morison, *Some Fruits of Theosophy*, is comparatively accurate when dealing with the Liberal Catholic Church itself but grossly inaccurate when dealing with other results of Mathew's movement.

of the Star of the East. The movement is not Christian in any normally accepted sense of the word, but is a combination of Roman Catholic ceremonial and Oriental occultism. The 'Presiding Bishop' of the body resides in England, and it has a small number of churches throughout the country, but only an insignificant following of lay people. There are also branches in India, America, Australia, the Dutch East Indies and on the Continent of Europe. The main strength of the movement numerically appears to be in America, though its spiritual centre is at Adyar in India. Although the movement is widespread, however, it is not numerically strong in any one place. It claims that its succession descends from Mathew, but, owing to the esoteric nature of its teachings, grave doubts must be expressed as to the validity of its Orders.

Prince de Landas, as has been stated, is responsible for two separate lines of succession in America. On October 3rd, 1916, he consecrated William Henry Francis Brothers, and on the following day consecrated Carmel Henry Carfora. The reason for the double consecration is very obscure, and the whole thing appears to have been done without Mathew's consent or approval. The streams have developed separately, each claiming to be the only true body of Old Catholics in America.

Brothers seems to have had a small following before his consecration. They are described as "a body of Benedictine monks, professing Old Catholic principles. These had been engaged in mission work all over the United States. These Benedictines were, on the 3rd October, 1911, received into union with the European Old Catholics and were placed under the jurisdiction of Mgr. Jan Francis Tichy, appointed Episcopal Administrator in America by the Archbishop of Utrecht, Dr. Gul, until such time as their Abbot, who had been elected Bishop, could receive the Episcopate."[1] These claims of being in communion with Utrecht are quite false,[2] but Brothers' sect is in communion with the Mariavite Church of Poland. According to their constitution, the Metropolitan See is New York, and the hierarchy in America shall consist of seven bishops, one of whom is to

[1] *The Story of the Old Catholic Church in America*, p. 11.

[2] The present Archbishop of Utrecht writes thus in answer to an inquiry regarding 'Mgr. Jan Francis Tichy': "Never was this man known by us, never was he acknowledged as bishop, nor—this not in the least—was he appointed for some mission by Mgr. Gul, the predecessor of my predecessor. We know nothing of these Benedictine monks professing Old Catholic principles."

be styled Archbishop, and the others Bishops-Auxiliary.[1] For some time the sect had its headquarters at 'St. Augustine's Abbey', Cos Cob, Connecticut, where the Prior was the late F. Bligh Bond, the Glastonbury archæologist. The 'Abbey' has since removed to New York.

Carfora's organisation is much more widespread, and it is claimed that it has representatives in France, Switzerland, Italy and Poland. In the last few years Carfora has performed a number of consecrations and apparently "founded" several new churches. Neither he nor Brothers is recognized by Mgr. B. M. Williams.

One of the most regrettable features of Mathew's episcopate was the founding of the Order of Corporate Reunion in 1908. This claimed to be a revival of Dr. F. G. Lee's earlier movement, but was in fact unconnected with it. By means of this Order Mathew offered ordination and consecration to such Anglican incumbents as might be disposed to accept it. The number of those who actually accepted these Orders was probably very small, and the few who did accept them were careful to keep the fact hidden. The Order seems still to exist in a shadowy underground way, though it has no connection with the legitimate Mathew succession as represented by Archbishop Williams. This Archbishop, in his first Pastoral Letter, stated his position quite clearly in regard to the matter: "I believe it to be fairly well known that I have never been in sympathy with the Order, and that I have never ordained one of its members. I propose to refuse Holy Orders on the lines of the Order of Corporate Reunion, while recognizing that I have a duty towards those ordained by my predecessors. . . ."[2] The numbers adhering to this Order are probably now such as might be counted on the fingers, but the very existence of such people raises natural questions as to their position. It is difficult to see how they reconcile their position in relation to the Church in which they openly minister, and whose revenues they do not scruple to accept. It is ecclesiastical anarchy, of which no good can possibly come, and it is much to be hoped that a way will be found of adequately dealing with the matter, and that legislation may be enacted for the removal of persons whose presence within the Anglican ministry is to its, and their, discredit.

[1] *The Story of the Old Catholic Church in America*, p. 19.

[2] *A Pastoral Letter for Advent*, 1920, by Bernard Mary, Archbishop of the old Roman Catholic Church in Great Britain, p. 8.

I

The Mathew Succession

Gerard Gul, Archbishop of Utrecht, on April 28th, 1908, consecrated

Arnold Harris Mathew, who, on April 14th, 1916, consecrated

Bernard Mary Williams[1] as his perpetual co-adjutor with right of succession.

II

Arnold Harris Mathew, on October 28th, 1914, consecrated

Frederick Samuel Willoughby,[2] who, on September 26th, 1915, consecrated

Bernard Edward Rupert Gauntlett and

Robert King.[3] On February 13th, 1916, Willoughby consecrated

James Ingall Wedgwood,[4] who, on July 22nd, 1916, consecrated

Charles Webster Leadbeater[5] as Bishop for Australia. On June 24th, 1917, Wedgwood consecrated

[1] Mgr. Williams was intended by Mathew to succeed him as head of the 'Old Roman Catholic (pro-Uniate) Rite in Great Britain,' and is consequently the only legitimate successor of Mathew's movement. He is theologically orthodox and, although his movement is extremely small, it has been entirely free from scandal since he succeeded to the headship of it. In one of his publications he asserts: "We disclaim all pretensions of being in any sense 'a Church.' We are simply a Rite within the Catholic Church" (*The History and Purpose of the Old Roman Catholic (pro-Uniate) Rite in Great Britain*, p. 12). In the same booklet he asserts that: "We accept the Faith precisely as it is defined by the Infallible Authority of the Holy See of Rome" (*ibid*). He has not yet consecrated a successor.

[2] A disreputable ex-Anglican who had been compelled to resign his cure when charged with crimes of gross sexual perversion. He represented himself to Mathew as one who was being persecuted by a Protestant bishop, and Mathew, unaware of the facts, consecrated him as 'Bishop of St. Pancras'. He was expelled from Mathew's movement before performing any consecrations, and finally died a Roman Catholic.

[3] Gauntlett and King were both theosophists. Gauntlett was secretary of the Theosophical Society Order of Healers. King was a consulting psychic.

[4] A theosophist who became first 'Presiding Bishop' of the 'Liberal Catholic Church'. From Wedgwood onwards all bishops in this line are Theosophists, and have no connection with any other Mathew line.

[5] Leadbeater had been connected with Mrs. Annie Besant's movement in India. His big book, *The Science of the Sacraments*, is the standard

THE JONKHEER JULIEN ADRIAN MAZEL[1] as Auxiliary Bishop for Australia. Wedgwood, on July 13th, 1919, consecrated

IRVING STEIGER COOPER[2] as Bishop for the U.S.A. On March 9th, 1924, Leadbeater consecrated

FRANK WATERS PIGOTT[3] as Regionary Bishop for Great Britain and Ireland. On May 18th, 1924, Leadbeater consecrated

JOHN ROSS THOMSON[4] as Suffragan Bishop for New Zealand. On June 29th, 1924, Leadbeater consecrated

JOHN WALKER[5] as Suffragan Bishop for South Africa. On August 4th, 1925, Leadbeater consecrated

GEORGE SYDNEY ARUNDALE.[6] Leadbeater, on May 23rd, 1926, consecrated

JOHN MOYNIHAN TETTEMER[7] as Auxiliary Bishop for the U.S.A. On July 18th, 1926, Wedgwood consecrated

EDWIN BURT BECKWITH[8] as Suffragan Bishop for U.S.A. On October 17th, 1926, Leadbeater consecrated

RAY MARSHALL WARDALL also as Suffragan Bishop for U.S.A. Wedgwood on January 29th, 1928, consecrated

ARTHUR GERALD HOUNSFIELD as Auxiliary Bishop for France. On April 18th, 1928, Wedgwood consecrated

JOHAN HUBERT BONJER[9] as Auxiliary Bishop for Holland. On August 15th, 1928, Wedgwood consecrated

---

work of the Liberal Catholic Church on all such subjects; it abounds in unhealthy mysticism and fantastic symbolism. He was originally in Anglican orders, but joined the Theosophical Society in 1883. He was elected Presiding Bishop of the Liberal Catholic Church in 1923, and died in 1934.

[1] He was appointed Regionary Bishop for the Netherlands Indies and in 1919 additionally for the Netherlands. He died in 1928.

Of the titles used by this body a 'Regionary Bishop' is ranked as an Archbishop of a Province; Suffragans are equivalent to diocesan bishops, and auxiliary bishops are much the same as bishops suffragan in the Church of England.

[2] Died in 1935.

[3] An ex-Anglican priest. He was elected Presiding Bishop in 1934, which position he still holds.

[4] Died in 1938.

[5] Resigned in 1934.

[6] Founder of the Order of the Star in the East, a society whose main function was to publicize the claims of J. Krishnamurti to be the "World Teacher" under the name of Alcyone. Arundale was appointed Regionary Bishop for India in 1926; he resigned in 1934 and became President of the Theosophical Society. He died in 1945.

[7] Formerly a Roman Catholic priest; appointed Suffragan Bishop for U.S.A. in 1927.

[8] Worked in Chicago and died in 1929.

[9] Resigned in 1935.

ADRIAAN GERARD VREEDE as Regionary Bishop for the Netherlands Indies. On August 15th, 1930, Leadbeater consecrated

JOHN CORDES[1] as Auxiliary Bishop for Europe and

WALDEMAR NYSSENS[2] also as Auxiliary Bishop for Europe. On September 13th, 1931, Cooper consecrated

CHARLES HAMPTON[3] as Auxiliary Bishop for U.S.A. Leadbeater, on May 14th, 1932, consecrated

DAVID MORTON TWEEDIE as Regionary Bishop for Australia, who, on February 24th, 1934, consecrated

WILLIAM CRAWFORD[4] as Auxiliary Bishop for New Zealand. On June 23rd, 1935, Hampton consecrated

EDMUND WALTER SHEEHAN as Auxiliary Bishop for U.S.A. Pigott, on August 9th, 1936, consecrated

BUENAVENTURA JIMENEZ as Suffragan Bishop for Puerto Rico. On August 23rd of the same year Pigott consecrated

FEDERICO JOSE FARIÑAS as Suffragan Bishop for Cuba. On September 6th, 1936, Vreede consecrated

FRANS LOUIS GERARD FOURNIER as Suffragan Bishop for the Netherlands Indies. Hampton, on February 7th, 1937, consecrated

JOSE BASILEIO ACUNA as Suffragan Bishop for Central America including Columbia. Pigott, on September 25th, 1938, consecrated

FRANÇOIS ANTOINE BRANDT as Auxiliary Bishop for the Netherlands. On May 28th, 1939, Tweedie consecrated

LAWRENCE WILFRED BURT as Auxiliary Bishop for Australia. Hampton, on July 2nd, 1939, consecrated

JOHN THEODORE ELKLUND as Auxiliary Bishop for U.S.A. Tweedie, on August 20th, 1939, consecrated

STANLEY SPROTT FISHER as Auxiliary Bishop for Australia.

There have been no consecrations since that of Fisher.

In 1922 a Liberal Catholic priest, F. E. Pearce, secured clandestine consecration from Willoughby. He remained a priest of the Liberal Catholic Church, not exercising his episcopate, which he appears to have obtained solely because he believed it would give him greater power in his healing work.

[1] Appointed Regionary Bishop for East Central Europe in 1935.

[2] Appointed Regionary Bishop for West Central Europe in 1935.

[3] Became Regionary Bishop in 1935 with residence in Los Angeles.

[4] Became Regionary Bishop in the same year.

III

Arnold Harris Mathew, on June 13th, 1910, consecrated
Herbert Ignatius Beale[1] and
Arthur William Howarth.[2]

IV

Arnold Harris Mathew, on January 7th, 1911, consecrated
Francis Herbert Bacon,[3] who consecrated, on December 2nd, 1914, in America,
Thomas Joseph Bensley,[4] who, in 1915, consecrated
Arthur Willoughby Henzell.[5]

V

Arnold Harris Mathew, on January 7th, 1911, consecrated
William Edmund Scott-hall,[6]
Cuthbert Francis Hinton[7] and
Frederick Clement Christie Egerton.[8]

[1] Beale had had an ' Old Catholic ' mission at Gunnersbury before Mathew was connected with the movement and had been prevailed upon to close it. He made several excursions between Canterbury and Rome, finally dying as Rector of Great Sutton, Essex. He did not propagate the succession.

[2] Howarth had been Roman Catholic parish priest at Corby, Grantham, and in 1909 was proceeded against by the Holy Office of the Inquisition on the charge, so he stated, of irregularities concerning Mass stipends (see his tract *A Protest against the Tyranny of the Roman Inquisition and of His Holiness Pope Pius X*). The Church of Rome excommunicated both Beale and Howarth in a decree dated February 11th, 1911. Howarth continued to reside at Corby until his death in 1942, but never exercised his Orders.

[3] Bacon had been an Anglican incumbent before joining Mathew's movement. For a short time after Mathew's death he acted as Archbishop in the illness of B. M. Williams. He was the prime mover in Mathew's Order of Corporate Reunion. He later returned to the Anglican Church and became incumbent of All Saints', Stepney; while holding that position he was imprisoned for grave moral offences. The direct succession from him seems to have come to an end.

[4] He later became Rector of St. Andrew's Episcopal Church, Lambertville, New Jersey.

[5] Formerly one of Mathew's priests; he is said to have officiated as an Anglican priest for some years.

[6] Now dead. At one time he had a place of worship in the parish of St. Thomas, Oxford, while at the same time acting as master in a Roman Catholic school elsewhere.

[7] Went to America, and worked afterwards as an Anglican priest in the diocese of Fond-du-Lac.

[8] Was reconciled with the Holy See, became a soldier and performed no ministerial functions.

VI

ARNOLD HARRIS MATHEW, on July 2nd, 1916, consecrated JAMES COLUMBA MCFALL[1] as Bishop for Ireland. McFall, on December 21st, 1933, consecrated
THOMAS REGINALD COATBRIDGE WILLIAMS.[2]

VII

FREDERICK SAMUEL WILLOUGHBY, on November 5th, 1916, consecrated
FREDERICK JAMES.[3] Willoughby, on July 9th, 1922, consecrated
JAMES BARTHOLOMEW BANKS,[4] who, in 1925, consecrated
PAUL FRANCIS COPE, of Kansas City, U.S.A., on May 28th, 1940, Banks consecrated an Anglican clergyman
SIDNEY ERNEST PAGE NEEDHAM who has now been re-consecrated by Newman of the Ferrete succession.

VIII

ARNOLD HARRIS MATHEW consecrated, probably on August 22nd, 1917,

[1] McFall comes from Ireland, where he carries on an antique business in Belfast, but he appears to function only in England. He is not recognised by the other Mathew bishops.

[2] Formerly Rector of Great Sutton in the diocese of Chelmsford, the advowson being in the possession of W. Noel Lambert (*vide infra*). Williams claims that he was consecrated to maintain the Mathew succession in England, though he asserts that he has not yet performed a consecration. On March 22, 1947, his appointment as Rector of Walton-le-Wolds, Leicester, was announced.

[3] James himself claims that this consecration was performed by Mathew, who had originally ordained him to the priesthood. He has a place of 'worship' in Basil Street, Knightsbridge, known as 'The Sanctuary'. In one of his leaflets he states: "The teaching given at the Sanctuary is not dogmatic; it is to be accepted only in so far as it may strike a responsive chord within the soul. The aim should be to demonstrate in one's own life that the Divine Laws, when understood and lived, lead to spiritual regeneration." In another leaflet it is stated: "The only creed of the Sanctuary is 'I believe in God' and it reduces all ethics to one of non-injury. There is no belief in any special divine revelation but revelation unfolds in the process of natural and spiritual evolution as the mind of man expands." The services are held behind locked doors and a certain part of the cult appears to centre in a figure of the god Apollo.

[4] Archbishop Banks at one time presided over an establishment in Maiden Lane, known as 'The Church of the Sacrifice'. Later he retired to Windsor, where he used the title of 'His Excellency the Patriarch of Windsor'. He now uses the title of 'His Excellency the Lord Patriarch Banks'. He is said to have received conditional re-consecration in the Ferrete succession.

William Noel Lambert and
John Arnold Carter.[1]

IX

American Succession

Arnold Harris Mathew, on June 29th, 1913, consecrated for work in Scotland
Prince de Landas, Berghes et de Rache,[2] who, however, went to America and, on October 3rd, 1916, consecrated
William Henry Francis Brothers, and on the day following
Carmel Henry Carfora. In 1927 de Landas consecrated
Stanislaus Mickiewicz.[3]

X

Carmel Henry Carfora,[4] on May 30th, 1921, consecrated

[1] It appears that the consecration of these Anglican clergymen was connected with the Order of Corporate Reunion founded by Mathew in 1908 as a revival of Dr. F. G. Lee's society (see pp. 63ff). This Order appears still to have a certain subterranean existence. There is some mystery attached to these consecrations owing to the fact that Mathew's Register was removed after his death by an unauthorized but interested party. Before his death Mathew gave Mgr. B. M. Williams a copy of the Register written in his own hand, and in which he states that he has performed no consecrations apart from those specified therein. In that copy neither of the above names appears, and there is therefore no available proof that these persons went through any form of consecration whatever. Furthermore, Mathew's episcopal seal was removed and not surrendered for the purpose of being defaced, so that a document bearing that seal would not in itself constitute proof of consecration. There is, however, adequate proof that these persons have claimed the episcopate. The name of Allen Hay is printed in a chart of the Mathew succession circulated by the Bishop Cope organisation (see p. 30), as having been consecrated by Mathew on December 19th, 1919. Little reliance can be placed on this document.

[2] Prince de Landas apparently had no commission from Mathew to perform any consecrations in America, but, on the other hand, he is described in *The Old Roman Catholic Almanack and Guide* for November, 1928, as " I Old Roman Catholic Archbishop of America ". He died in 1920.

[3] Formerly a priest of the Polish National Catholic Church. He was deposed by de Landas and Carfora in December, 1918, and died in 1923. See tables X—XIV.

[4] An Italian by birth, and originally a Roman Catholic priest. He claims to be a Doctor of Philosophy of the University of Naples and a Doctor of Theology of the Theological University of Naples. He now describes himself as " the most Illustrious Lord, the Supreme Primate of the North American Old Catholic Church." In the *Year Book of American Churches* for 1939 it is stated that he has 27 churches and 11,109

Instrumentum Consecrationis

Reverendissimi Domini [illegible]

In Episcopum

In Nomine Sanctissimae et Individuae Trinitatis. Amen.

Anno Domini [illegible] Episcopatus Sui iv, Die [illegible] mensis [illegible]

Illustrissimus ac Reverendissimus Dominus Rodolphus Franciscus Edouarus St. Patricius Alphonsus Ghislain de Gramont Hamilton de Lorraine, Archiepiscopus Ecclesiae Veteris Romanae Catholicae Americae, Princeps de Landas-Berghes St. Winock et de Rache (de Lorraine Brabant) in capella Archiepiscopi Waukeganensis III, intra Missarum Solemnia in Episcopum Ecclesiae Veteris Romanae Americae, REVERENDISSIMUM DOMINUM [illegible] Presbyterum dictae Ecclesiae, in synodo Catholicorum ejusdem Ecclesiae Episcopum electum, juxta ritum PONTIFICALE ROMANUM praescriptum Ordinavit et Consecravit, Assistentibus et Co-operantibus Illustrissimis Dominis [illegible]

ACTA SUNT HAEC IN PRAEFATO ANNO MENSE AC DIE SUPRA DICTIS PRAESENTIBUS IBIDEM TESTIBUS INFRA SIGNATUS

+ [illegible] Archiepiscopus

INSTRUMENT OF CONSECRATION OF CARMEL HENRY CARFORA.

[To face p. 24.

ROMAN W. SLOCINSKI.[1] On February 11th, 1924, Carfora consecrated

EDWIN WALLACE HUNTER[2] as Regionary Bishop for the United States and Canada. On September 21st, 1926, Carfora consecrated

CHARLES ALPHONSE BLANCHETTE as 'Bishop of Portland'. On May 7th, 1929, Carfora consecrated

WILLIAM S. HAMMOND.[3] On December 15th, 1929, Carfora consecrated

HARRY FREDERICK VAN TRUMP[4] as 'Missionary Archbishop.' On December 15th, 1929, Carfora consecrated

PAMPHILE CYRIL DEPEW[5] as 'Archbishop of Chicago.' On November 21st, 1930, Carfora consecrated

HENRY PETER RIEL,[6] while on November 29th, 1931, he consecrated

BASIL DRAPAK[7] as Archbishop of the 'Ukranian Orthodox Church' which he had founded. On December 8th, 1940, Carfora consecrated

JOHN RICHARD WELD[8] and

---

followers, but these figures are very doubtful. Carfora appears to claim some sort of infallibility, since in one of his publications it is stated: " The Supreme Primate is recognised as the Spiritual Head of the Church. All doctrinal laws or new articles of faith shall be considered final when he speaks *ex cathedra* . . . He shall have full and exclusive jurisdiction over the whole Church in all matters ecclesiastical, civil and temporal " (*General Constitution and Bye-Laws of the North American Old Catholic Church*, p. 7). He was at one time in communion with B. M. Williams, who later excommunicated him and all in communion with him.

[1] Later deposed, restored and deposed again in the five years that followed; now dead.

[2] Formerly an Anglican. He became ' Archbishop ' in 1929, and died in 1942. His body was called ' The Holy Catholic Church of the Apostles in the Diocese of Louisiana '. So far as is known has left no successors.

[3] Carfora later quarrelled with Hammond and deposed him. He has a chapel with a small following in Detroit and a mission in Windsor, Ontario.

[4] Later deposed by Carfora. He was thoroughly disreputable, and died in the late 1930's.

[5] An ex-Roman priest; in 1930 he abandoned his title in Carfora's organisation and later rejoined the Roman Church, was sent to a monastery and has not been heard of since.

[6] Consecrated for work in Michigan, but has been completely inactive for years.

[7] Died in 1937; his Ukranian following is now under the bishops of the Russian-American Synod.

[8] Now completely inactive in the Carfora organisation and a soldier in the American Army.

Francis Xavier Resch.[1] On April 16th, 1941, Carfora consecrated

Richard Arthur Marchenna.[2] On July 30th, 1942, Carfora consecrated

Herbert Augustin Rogers.[3] In 1943 Carfora founded the 'Protestant Orthodox Western Church', and on August 15th of that year consecrated as bishop of it

Frederick Littler Pyman.[4] On December 8th, 1943, Carfora consecrated

Alfred Thomas Bennett Haines.[5] In 1944 Carfora consecrated

James F. Cyrus for negro work in New York City. Also in 1944 Carfora consecrated

Sigismund K. Vipartas as a Lithuanian bishop. On April 20th, 1945, Carfora consecrated

Paul A. R. Markiewicz[6] and

Francis Mazur[7]. On June 17th, 1945, Carfora consecrated

Earl Anglin Lawrence James to be ' Bishop of Toronto '. In November, 1946, Carfora consecrated

Charles G. Vestle.

XI

Carmel Henry Carfora, on June 12th, 1921, consecrated

[1] He was deposed by the Carfora bishops in 1942, and has since entered into affiliation with Paul Francis Cope of Kansas City who was consecrated by Banks of the Mathew succession.

[2] A negro of Jersey City, where he has no organised following or church. He has been suspended at least twice by Carfora.

[3] A West Indian negro; he was originally a bishop in a faction of the African Orthodox Church (see p. 37), then left it and was received by Carfora in 1941 and given conditional re-consecration by him in the following year. He has recently been made " Archbishop of New York " by Carfora, and is pastor of the St. Augustine Old Roman Catholic Church in New York City.

[4] He has a following of Lutheran Independents in California.

[5] Originally ordained priest by Willoughby in 1915. In 1920 he received Anglican priest's orders from the Bishop of London; later he emigrated to Canada and became ' Vicar General ' of the Liberal Catholic Church there. He is now, with Carfora's approval, working as a Congregational minister in Pittsburgh.

[6] Markiewicz comes from Canada, where his following is called ' The Apostolic Catholic Polish Church of Canada '. For a quarter of a century he acted as bishop without having received any form of episcopal consecration; later, according to a Carfora report, " having made his submission to our Church, was accepted with all his followers in bona fide communion " (*American National Catholic*, May, 1945).

[7] Formerly a Roman Catholic priest; he was consecrated to serve under Markiewicz, and such work as he has is in Chicago.

SAMUEL DURLIN BENEDICT.[1] In January, 1927, Benedict consecrated
GEORGE AUGUSTUS NEWMARK.[2]

XII

CARMEL HENRY CARFORA, on March 19th, 1931, consecrated
JAMES CHRISTIAN CRUMMEY[3] and
MATHER WILLIAMS SHERWOOD.[4] On May 11th, 1941, Crummey consecrated
MURRAY ANDREW LEE BURNETT[5] as 'Missionary Bishop of the Universal Christian Communion for Baltimore, Md., and adjacent states of the S.E. United States'.

[1] Benedict was deposed by Carfora on January 24th, 1927, apparently for performing the consecration of Newmark. He then founded what he called ' The Evangelical Catholic Church ', which claimed, in *The Year Book of American Churches*, to have 137 churches, and 27,400 members, which is probably five hundred times the actual figure. Benedict died in 1945.

[2] Newmark originally operated under Benedict's ' Evangelical Catholic Church ', but later apparently split from Benedict and had his followers registered as an autonomous unit, which he described as ' The American Old Catholic Church ', and which functioned in Louisiana, Maryland and other southern States. At one time he claimed over a thousand followers, but he died in 1939 or 1940, leaving two priests and very few people, and these have put themselves under Bishop Crummey of the Universal Christian Communion. There are certain shadowy persons in America who claim to have been consecrated either by Benedict or Newmark, but it is virtually certain that neither did, in fact, leave any episcopal progeny.

[3] Crummey had organised the ' Universal Episcopal Communion ' in 1930, which was a movement intended to reform and bring order into the scattered organizations in America and elsewhere claiming to be Old Catholic. It was founded " to establish a conciliar body of bishops to unite the then badly divided body of Old Catholics in North America and the world. Subsidiary to the Universal Episcopal Communion, which existed as an episcopal council, the Universal Christian Communion was instituted as an ecclesiastical body into which the several small and separated Old Catholic churches in North America and elsewhere might be united. The two bodies, separately named, are, in reality, one body, the bishops having the name Universal Episcopal Communion for their separate episcopal existence and functioning." This movement demands a higher standard of discipline than that which obtains among the other so-called Old Catholic organisations in America and, in general, its bishops appear to be men of greater worth. Crummey is the primate of the two bodies, and in 1944 he withdrew from all relations of ecclesiastical comity with Carfora. For a note of the Universal Episcopal Communion see *New York World-Telegram,* Oct. 28, 1933, p. 20.

[4] Served with Crummey from 1931 to 1940, when he resigned and retired from all ecclesiastical functions.

[5] Originally one of Newmark's priests.

XIII

Carfora Succession in Mexico

Carmel Henry Carfora, on October 17th, 1926, consecrated
José Joachin Perez y Budar[1] as 'Archbishop of Mexico City',
Antonio Benigno Lopez y Sierra[2] as Coadjutor, and
José Macario Lopez[3] as 'Bishop of Pueblo, Mex.'. On December 24th, 1929, Carfora consecrated
Hieronymus Maria as 'Bishop of San Antonio, Texas'. On June 26th, 1932, Carfora consecrated
Armin von Monte de Honor[4] and
Vincente José Linan.[5] Some time before the end of 1933 Perez y Budar consecrated
José Emeterio Valdez and
José Edwardo Davila-Garcia.[6] On February 26th, 1933, Carfora consecrated
Francisco José Duran de la Vega as 'Bishop of the State of Vera Cruz'. On June 29th, 1933, Carfora consecrated
Josephus Petrus Ortiz as 'Primate of the Mexican Old Roman Catholic Church'.

XIV

William Henry Francis Brothers[7] in June, 1918, consecrated

[1] Now deceased, and said to have been reconciled with the Holy See on his death-bed.

[2] Later deposed, and now apparently dead.

[3] Now apparently inactive.

[4] Lives in Mexico City, but as a foreign-born Mexican citizen, unable to function ecclesiastically.

[5] After a short stay in Mexico moved to San Antonio, Texas. Later he quarrelled with the Mexican Old Roman Catholic leaders, and with Carfora, and was suspended. He is now dead.

[6] In a list of clergy in 1933 he is listed as " Archbishop and Patriarch ", but later the Carfora affiliates rejected him and chose a new Archbishop.

In the 1933 list Angel R. Perez and Jose N. Cortez-Villasenor are also listed as bishops, but there is no information as to the dates of their consecrations.

[7] Brothers had already formed a small sect when he was consecrated by de Landas, and this he took with him when he was dismissed. His dismissal by de Landas appears to have been on the grounds that at the time of the consecration he had not, in fact, received the Orders of deacon and priest. It appears that, at de Landas' request, he was never recognised by the Mathew bishops in England. He now calls himself ' Archbishop Francis ', ' Archbishop of the Old Catholic Church in America ' (the sect is also variously styled ' Catholic Church of

ANTONIO RODRIGUEZ as Auxiliary Bishop for the Portuguese. On March 9th, 1924, Brothers consecrated

ALBERT EDWARD SELCER[1] and on March 14th of the same year

ALBERTUS JEHAN as Regionary Bishop of Chicago. Early in 1925 a Bishop of the Syrian Church,

JOSEPH ZIELONKO, was received into Brothers' sect, and he assisted Brothers to consecrate

WILLIAM MONTGOMERY BROWN[2] as Auxiliary Bishop in succession to Bishop Stanislaus Mickiewicz. In the 1930's Brothers consecrated

ALBERT D. BELL.[3] Bell consecrated

EDGAR P. VEROSTEK.

XV

ALLEGED MATHEW SUCCESSION THROUGH WHITMAN[4]

ARNOLD HARRIS MATHEW, on June 8th, 1910, is said to have consecrated

---

North America' and 'Orthodox Old Catholic Church in America'). Brothers resides at what he describes as a 'Benedictine Abbey' which was for many years in New York, but has recently moved. In this establishment a position is found for his wife.

1 Formerly a Vilatte priest, and now a priest of the Protestant Episcopal Church.

2 Brown had been Bishop of Arkansas of the Protestant Episcopal Church. He resigned jurisdiction in 1919, and in 1925 was deprived for heresy. He was at one time connected with a small body in Denver, Colorado, styled 'The Liberal Church', and *The Rocky Mountain News* in October, 1925, announced that he had accepted membership in it, the announcement being made by a certain 'Bishop' Frank H. Rice, who elsewhere in the same paper described himself as 'Commissioner of God', and who appears to have been mentally unbalanced. Brown ceased to be a Christian and for some time styled himself 'the atheist bishop'. He died in the early 1930's.

3 Bell at one time functioned as a bishop of the Carfora Church, having, according to a statement of Carfora, represented himself as having been consecrated by Bishop Kreuzer of Bonn. He was later dismissed by Carfora.

4 No evidence for the existence of this line of succession before 1940 is to be found among any of the documents or accounts of the late Bishop Mathew, and Whitman's consecration appears to be denied by all the Mathew bishops, while his name is not contained in the copy of the Register possessed by Mgr. Williams. It is stated that Whitman was consecrated in order to perform episcopal functions in connection with the Llanthony foundation of Father Ignatius, and not for work in connection with Mathew's own movement. The line from Cope certainly exists, but its claim to descend from Mathew, or even from Whitman, must remain a matter of dispute until further evidence is forthcoming.

RALPH WHITMAN[1] as 'Bishop for Llanthony Abbey', who, on July 19th, 1940, is said to have consecrated

ERNEST ODELL COPE[2] as 'Bishop of the Order of Llanthony Brothers'. Cope, on August 2nd, 1942, consecrated

JAMES YORKE BATLEY.[3] On June 18th, 1944, Cope consecrated

JOHN SYER as 'Bishop of Llanthony', who, on July 23rd, 1944, consecrated

FRANCIS ERNEST LANGHELT,[4] otherwise known as 'Francis, Bishop of Minster'.

[1] Whitman is said to have migrated to Canada shortly after his consecration, and only to have returned to England at the beginning of the late war. A printed document which purports to be a Pastoral Letter from him, entitled *An Open Letter to British Old Catholics*, is dated from Gloucester on Advent Sunday, 1940. In this document the claim is made that he is " the senior Old Catholic Bishop in the United Kingdom ", and it continues: " All Bishops, Priests and other Clergy in Old Catholic Orders are reminded of their duty of canonical obedience, and must submit themselves to my jurisdiction ". There is, however, no evidence that this document actually emanated from Whitman and, indeed, there is no evidence that such a person as Whitman actually exists.

[2] It is clear, of course, that Cope's claim to the episcopate cannot be in any sense accepted until the mystery regarding his consecrator is cleared up. He possesses a document which purports to be a certificate of consecration, but its seal is indecipherable and in itself there is nothing to show that it is genuine.

[3] Formerly one of Vernon Herford's priests.

[4] Syer and Langhelt have both received conditional re-consecration from de Willmott Newman of the Ferrete succession.

CERTIFICATE OF CONSECRATION

+

In the Name of God. Amen.

WE, Ralph Whitman, Regionary Old Catholic Bishop for Wales, consecrated by the late Archbishop Mathew on the 8th day of June 1910 as Bishop for Llanthony Abbey, Do Hereby Certify that for the purpose of re-establishing the monastic vocation at Llanthony (which has been lying in abeyance since the death of the late Father Ignatius) and providing spiritual ministrations for The Order of Llanthony Abbey Brothers, We did on the 19th day of July 1940 at Repton, by the laying-on of Hands with Prayer and Anointing, Apostolically Consecrate to the Office of a Bishop in the One Holy Catholic and Apostolic Church of Jesus Christ Ernest Odell Cope, whom We had previously ordained Priest on the 11th day of July 1939 at Gloucester.

As Witness Our Signature and Seal this 19th day of July 1940.

Ralph Whitman +
Regionary Bishop

Witnesses:-

Harold Sugden
Thomas Heath
Thomas Frederick Appleby.
Robert Edmund Langton
James Walter Slater

ALLEGED INSTRUMENT OF CONSECRATION OF ERNEST ODELL COPE.

[To face p. 30.

CHAPTER IV

THE VILATTE SUCCESSION

JOSEPH RENÉ VILATTE was a Parisian who early migrated to America and was originally trained for the Roman Catholic priesthood, but on leaving the Roman Church was for a short time admitted to membership of the Methodist body in Montreal. During the following years his changes of religious affiliation were numerous and bewildering. He four times returned to the Roman Catholic Church, once to the Methodists, became a Congregationalist minister and twice a Presbyterian. The last excursion into Presbyterianism was made under the influence of Pastor Chiniquy. He then, in 1885, when still only thirty-one, approached the Anglican Bishop of Fond du Lac, Dr. Hobart Brown, with a view to admission into the priesthood of the Protestant Episcopal Church. At Dr. Brown's suggestion he started work among the Belgian Old Catholics in Wisconsin and, to facilitate this work, was sent for ordination to Dr. Herzog, Old Catholic Bishop in Switzerland, who conferred upon him the orders of deacon and priest in June, 1885. Vilatte took his oaths of canonical obedience, however, not to Dr. Herzog, but to the Bishop of Fond du Lac. The American House of Bishops permitted him to use the French Liturgy of the Christian Catholic Church at Berne in his mission.

For some time Vilatte appears to have done good work in this mission, but at the time of Dr. Brown's death in 1888 he was intriguing with the Old Catholics with a view to being consecrated bishop. Dr. Grafton, who succeeded Dr. Brown in the See of Fond du Lac, dissuaded the Old Catholics from taking this step and refused Vilatte's suggestion that he should consecrate him as 'Bishop-Abbot' of the American Old Catholics.[1] Vilatte then applied to the Russian Archbishop Vladimir for consecration and, when this was refused, applied to the Roman Catholic Bishop of Milwaukee, who likewise refused him. He repudiated the jurisdiction of Bishop Grafton and, on March 21st, 1892, was degraded from the priesthood and excommunicated by the Protestant Episcopal Church. At this time Vilatte called himself

[1] See Grafton, *A Journey Godward*, pp. 169ff.

'Supérieur de l'Eglise vieille-catholique d'Amerique'. He had already, apparently, been granted some sort of recognition by the Russian Archbishop Vladimir, who is said to have written the following declaration from San Francisco on May 9th, 1891:

"By the grace of God and the authority which the apostolic succession gives me, I, Vladimir, Bishop of the Orthodox Catholic Church, make known to all the clergy of the different denominations, and to all the Old Catholics, that the Reverend Father J. René Vilatte, Superior of the Old Catholic parish of Dyckesville (Wisconsin) is an orthodox Old Catholic, under the patronage of our Church, and that no one, be he bishop or priest, has the right to interdict or suspend him from his religious functions, except the Synod of the Russian Church; and that all action contrary to this declaration is null and invalid, according to liberty of conscience and the laws of this country. Vladimir, Bishop of the Greco-Russian Orthodox Church."[1]

Vilatte claimed to have been elected to the episcopate by the Old Catholics themselves. "It soon became obvious," says one of his supporters, "that an Old Catholic Bishop was as necessary for the life and development of the movement (i.e. in America) as an Old Catholic priesthood had been for its formation. . . . The need of a bishop became so pressing, that a Synod, representing all the actual Old Catholic families, met at Duvall, and in due canonical form elected Père Vilatte their future bishop, entreating him to obtain an *indisputable* episcopal consecration as soon as possible."[2]

Bishop Grafton comments thus on this 'synod': "The story that he was elected to the Bishopric of the Old Catholics is simply this: He carried around a paper amongst the few poor, ignorant people under his charge, which he demanded they should sign. Most of them complied, some of them being little children. There is only one clergyman's name on the petition and that, according to the statement of the clergyman so named, was forged."[3]

Following his degradation and excommunication Vilatte met a man called Harding, an ex-Roman Catholic of bad

[1] Quoted, Parisot, *Monseigneur Vilatte, Fondateur de l'Eglise vieille-catholique aux Etats-Unis d'Amérique*, pp. 23 24. But there exists no evidence that this is a genuine document and, indeed, its phraseology at several points argues against its genuineness.

[2] *The Genesis of Old Catholicism in America*, by 'Brother William, O.S.B.', p. 7.

[3] Bishop Grafton's statements were printed very fully in the *Church Review*.

life, and from him learnt of the condition of affairs in Ceylon, where some five thousand Latins,[1] who had broken away from the Roman Church in 1886, were under a certain 'Archbishop Alvares' of the 'Independent Catholic Church of Ceylon'. There is some mystery as to the exact status of Alvares. Mr. Donald Attwater, writing from the Roman Catholic point of view, describes him as a "Portuguese schismatical priest who had been consecrated bishop by the Jacobite Bishop of Kottayam in Malabar,[2] and put by the Jacobite Patriarch in charge of a number of schismatic Latin Catholics in Ceylon."[3] Alvares' consecration took place on July 29th, 1889, and in several of the booklets issued by the sects which claim descent from Vilatte it is stated that the Bishop of Kottayam acted as Legate of the Patriarch Ignatius Peter III at this consecration. However this may be, Vilatte went to Ceylon and, concealing his history as well as he was able, was consecrated, after some delay, by Alvares, on May 29th, 1892. Alvares himself, though under the protection of the Antiochene Patriarchate, was probably what we should understand by an *episcopus vagans*; he wrote to Father Ignatius of Llanthony as follows:

"Nearly a year elapsed since the application of the Old Catholics of America to consecrate Mgr. Vilatte and the sanction of the Holy See of Antioch thereon. The pros and cons were fully investigated in Ceylon, Malabar and Antioch, and it was after mature deliberation that the sanction for consecration was granted. Mgr. Vilatte, who did not expect such crucial test, reached Ceylon before the investigation was over, and he had thus to wait over nine months in the island."[4]

It is not likely that either in Antioch or Malabar at this time there existed adequate facilities for investigating the antecedents of a clergyman of an obscure mission in America, and there is more than a hint that the whole affair was 'managed' by Vilatte and Alvares.[5] It is claimed that the consecration was performed on the authority of a Bull of Ignatius Peter III of Antioch.

The alleged Bull of Ignatius Peter III has been the matter of considerable controversy. The original Syriac document appears to have been seen by no one trustworthy person. Bishops of the Vilatte succession have been con-

[1] The numbers are given by Parisot and may not be reliable.

[2] Mar Paul Athanasius.

[3] *Father Ignatius of Llanthony*, p. 141.

[4] *The Church Review*, Jan. 12th, 1899.

[5] For a good account of the See of Antioch a little before this time see Parry, *Six Months in a Syrian Monastery*.

stantly challenged to produce it, and have constantly failed to do so, though several alleged translations are in existence.[1] In view of the claims that are being built in some quarters upon this Bull, its non-appearance is bound to raise queries and suspicion.

His Grace Mar Julius, Representative of the Jacobite Patriarch in South India, has, however, stated in a letter that the following are the facts so far as he knows them, though he can produce no recorded evidence:

"(1) Father Xavier Alvares, a Latinite priest, joined our Church about the year 1888. The Metropolitan of Malabar at that time wrote to His Holiness the Patriarch of Antioch and received special sanction to consecrate him bishop. And in accordance with the rites of the Syrian Church the Metropolitan of Malabar consecrated him under the title of Mar Julius Alvares.

"(2) Vilatte was consecrated by Mar Julius assisted by the Metropolitans of Malabar. For the consecration the sanction was sought and duly received from the Patriarch.

"(3) The Canon Laws of the Syrian Church do not allow a Bishop alone to consecrate another bishop. But this Vilatte, possessing thus no power to consecrate bishops, began in violation of our canon laws to consecrate bishops. When this news reached the Patriarch of Antioch he excommunicated him, but even afterwards he is said to have 'consecrated' more 'bishops'. These 'bishops' 'consecrated' others and thus a Vilatte succession exists.

"(4) Orders conferred by Vilatte are *not* recognised as valid either by the Patriarch or by the Synod. Vilatte and his followers being under the ban of excommunication are not accepted into communion with the Church. They are alien to our Church.

"(5) The position of the Syrian Antiochene Church with regard to a person receiving consecration at the hands of a deposed bishop is that beside the fact that he is committing sin, he is considered completely devoid of Orders.

"(6) If such a bishop is to be received into communion he must be reconsecrated after proper repentance."

During the General Convention of the Protestant Episcopal Church in 1892 the House of Bishops considered the

[1] The writer possesses a photostatic copy of what purports to be the original translation of this Bull in the handwriting of the Secretary of the Metropolitan of Malabar and signed by the Metropolitan, but no Syriac authority will commit himself on the subject of the signature's genuineness. (See frontispiece of this book.)

matter, and Dr. Doane, Bishop of Albany, presented the following report, and the two resolutions were adopted:

"It appears that the bishops from whom M. Vilatte claims to have received consecration belonged to a body which is separated from Catholic Christendom because of its non-acceptance of the dogmatic decrees of the Council of Chalcedon as to our Blessed Lord's Person;

"These bishops had no jurisdiction or right to ordain a bishop for any part of the diocese under the charge of the Bishop of Fond du Lac;

"M. Vilatte was never elected by any duly accredited Synod.

"It appears that M. Vilatte, in seeking the Episcopate, made statements not warranted by the facts of the case, and seemed willing to join in with any body, Old Catholic, Greek, Roman, or Syrian, which would confer it upon him.

"More than two months before the time of his so-called consecration, he had been deposed from the sacred ministry.

"In view of these facts we propose the following resolutions:

"*Resolved*, That, in the opinion of this House, the whole proceedings in connection with the so-called consecration of J. René Vilatte were null and void, and that this Church does not recognise that any Episcopal character was thereby conferred.

"*Resolved*, That a statement of the above-recited facts be sent to the Archbishop of Utrecht, to the Old Catholics of Germany and Switzerland, and to the Metropolitans and Primates of the Anglican Communion."

In the summer of 1898 Vilatte came to England, and created some sensation by ordaining Father Ignatius of Llanthony to the priesthood. A few weeks after this event he sought reconciliation with the Holy See, but while his case was actually *sub judice*, he started what he called an "Italian National Episcopal Church" at Milan, and for this purpose consecrated Don Miraglia Gulotti as "Bishop of Piacenza". The reply of the Holy See was to place both Vilatte and Gulotti under major excommunication by a decree dated June 13th, 1900, wherein it is stated that they had incurred the sentence "iterum iterumque multiplici ex causa". Vilatte thereafter returned to America, and for the next fifteen years remained more or less inactive until his consecration of F. E. J. Lloyd in 1915. It was in this year, too, that Vilatte's movement was incorporated under the laws of the State of Illinois as 'The American Catholic Church', the incorporators being Vilatte himself, Lloyd and a certain Rev. Louis Zawistowski.

At a synod of his clergy in April, 1920, Vilatte expressed his desire to retire in favour of Lloyd. "Accordingly, at the same synod, Dr. Lloyd was unanimously chosen Archbishop while Archbishop Vilatte was accorded the honorary title of Exarch, and it was understood that the latter would practically retire from active service."[1] Shortly after this event Vilatte departed for France, and in 1925 was finally reconciled with the Holy See, and until the time of his death in 1929 resided at the Abbey of Pont Colbert, near Versailles.

Various successions descend from Vilatte, of which the two most widespread appear to be the American Catholic Church under Lloyd and his successors, and the African Orthodox Church, which descends from G. A. McGuire, who was consecrated by Vilatte in 1921.

Lloyd had originally been an Anglican priest, ordained by the Bishop of Oxford (Mackarness) for Newfoundland in 1882. While in Newfoundland he worked at the Flower's Cove Mission in the Straits of Belle Isle, but his record there was bad. From Newfoundland he went to America, and worked as a priest of the Protestant Episcopal Church, being subsequently nominated for a bishopric, but when the American House of Bishops inquired into his record they refused to elect him. He then became a Roman Catholic for a time, and finally joined Vilatte's movement. Lloyd was very active, and carried on a considerable work of proselytization; the spread of the 'American Catholic Church', from 1920 until his death in 1933, is largely due to his initiative.

In 1925 the Vilatte bodies under Lloyd and the Mathew succession through Carfora entered into some sort of union with one another in a synod convened by Carfora at Chicago.[2] The two sects appear to have united in some degree, though each preserved its own succession. They agreed to adopt 'The Holy Catholic Church in America' as the general title of the body, but leaving each branch the right to preserve its own distinctive title—viz., the American Catholic Church (Lloyd), the Old Roman Catholic Church (Carfora), the Polish Catholic Church (Boryzsewski) and others. They also agreed to the publication of a joint periodical to be

[1] Art. 'Status of the American Catholic Church' by Bishop Daniel [Hinton] in *The American Churchman*, vol. II, p. 9.

[2] There is an account of this synod in *The Catholic American*, Sept., 1925.

called *The Catholic American*. It is doubtful, however, whether this fusion was ever properly implemented except on paper; it is a fact no longer.

Early in September, 1921, a group of Negro Churchmen organised the 'African Orthodox Church' and George Alexander McGuire was consecrated by Vilatte as its first bishop. This body is situated mainly in the Southern States, and has also spread to South Africa. In America it numbered 3,200 in 1939, but by that time its main force was probably spent. The movement was as much a racial as a religious one. Its main period of advance was in 1922–23, when the Marcus Garvie Movement was reaching its climax. Throughout America there was a general awakening of racial consciousness, and negroes were clamouring for negro leadership in all departments of life. The Church was no exception. The African Orthodox Church claimed to offer to negro churchmen the emancipation they desired. It offered a negro Primacy, negro bishops and other high ecclesiastical offices which were denied them in the Episcopal Church. For a time this high-sounding ecclesiastical nomenclature worked like magic upon the childish imaginations of hundreds of American negroes. Now, however, the Garvie wave of racial enthusiasm has subsided, and the African Orthodox Church no longer possesses any magical charm for the members of the Episcopal Church, and offers little or no appeal to members of other denominational groups.

The body also invaded the Diocese of Nassau in the Bahama Islands, where it has a mission of some 175 members, but is quite without influence.

In 1927 McGuire consecrated Daniel William Alexander as 'Primate of the Province of South Africa'. Alexander resides at Beaconsfield, near Kimberley, but his adherents appear to be mainly in Kenya and Uganda. In 1931–32 he went to Uganda at the request of some Africans, and remained there about a year and a half. Whilst there he ordained a 'Vicar Apostolic', by name Reuben Spata, and a few deacons, all of whom, and the majority of their adherents, were people who have left the Anglican Church at some time or other. These have now mainly seceded from Alexander and look to the Pope and Patriarch of Alexandria, and have, in fact, sent two deacons to be trained in Egypt. Alexander's adherents in Uganda now number about five thousand, with one priest, five deacons and possibly thirty to fifty teachers. In Kenya his following is somewhat larger, consisting mainly of Africans who have left the Presbyterian Church owing to its action some years ago with regard to female circumcision. In the neighbourhood of Kimberley, where he lives, his following consists of a mere handful. Alexander was originally a member of a separatist body known as 'the African Churches', and his present followers in Beaconsfield appear to consist mainly of those who followed him when he was dismissed at its annual conference in 1924. It is believed that the funds for the building of his church at Beaconsfield were supplied by Marcus Garvie, though Alexander denies connection with any political organisation.

The Vilatte succession entered England originally through Gulotti, and this line has a living representative in Bishop Stannard, who is not only reputable and orthodox, but has shown no sign of perpetuating the succession. Another line of succession from Vilatte entered England through the activities of Churchill Sibley, an Englishman consecrated by Lloyd for work in this country. Sibley consecrated a Gold Coast native of the Fanti tribe called Anderson, who, in turn, consecrated F. C. A. Harrington.[1] Harrington was the first, apparently, to conceive the idea of undergoing a series of reconsecrations at the hands of various prelates from different successions, with a view to uniting the various *episcopi vagantes* under himself. For this purpose he was re-consecrated in 1938 by Heard of the Ferrete succession. Dorian Herbert, the only surviving bishop consecrated by Harrington, and so-called 'Bishop of Caerleon', has since been conditionally re-consecrated by de Willmott Newman of the Ferrete succession. There is perhaps no need to point out the grave theological fallacy implicit in such a performance, grounded, presumably, on a confusion between the powers conferred by consecration and those conferred by jurisdiction. There is also the apparent supposition that a man is consecrated bishop of a particular stream of succession rather than as a bishop of the Church of God.

I

The Vilatte Succession

Mar Paul Athanasius, Syrian Antiochene Bishop of Kottayam, on July 29th, 1889, consecrated

[1] An account of this consecration is in *The Hornsey Journal*, Sept. 13th, 1935, but clearly supplied by an interested party.

JULIUS ALVARES as 'Archbishop of the Independent Catholic Church of Goa and Ceylon'. Alvares, on May 29th, 1892, consecrated

JOSEPH RENÉ VILATTE as 'Archbishop of North America'. Vilatte, on September 9th, 1898, consecrated a Polish priest

STEPHEN KAMINSKI.[1] On May 6th, 1900, Vilatte consecrated

PAOLO MIRAGLIA GULOTTI as 'Bishop of Piacenza' who, on June 14th, 1903, consecrated

HENRY MARSH MARSH-EDWARDS[2] as 'Bishop of Caerleon', who, on June 15th, 1903, consecrated

HENRY BERNARD VENTHAM.[3] On December 27th, 1908, Gulotti consecrated

WILLIAM WHITEBROOK, who, on April 7th, 1912, consecrated

BASIL MAURICE STANNARD as 'Bishop of Walsingham'.[4]

II

THE GALLICAN AND GERMAN SUCCESSION

PAOLO MIRAGLIA GULOTTI, on December 4th, 1904, consecrated

JULIUS HUSSAY as Bishop of the 'Gallican Church'. Hussay, on June 21st, 1911, consecrated

LOUIS FRANÇOIS GIRAUD, who, on May 5th, 1918, consecrated

V. BLANCHARD. On December 28th, 1921, Giraud consecrated

PIERRE GASTON VIGNÉ.[5] Vigné, on June 3rd, 1924, consecrated

[1] Kaminski was forthwith excommunicated by the Roman Catholic Church, abandoned by Vilatte, and appears to have left no succession.

[2] Marsh-Edwards had been an Anglican incumbent, but had been cited to appear before the Consistory Court of the diocese of Southwell to answer charges against his moral character, and was by that Court pronounced ' incapable of holding preferment '. For a time he had a small church at Bournemouth, which he was compelled to close through lack of support.

[3] Ventham took the title of ' Bishop of Dorchester '. At the time of his consecration he was acting as an Anglican lay reader in Somerset and posing elsewhere as a Roman Catholic layman. He later received conditional re-ordination up to, and including, the priesthood, from Mathew. He died in 1944 as an Anglican incumbent.

[4] Bishop Stannard is the sole survivor of this line; he has a few priests who acknowledge his jurisdiction.

[5] Vigné had been an Old Catholic priest ordained by Bishop Herzog.

ALOYSIUS STUMPFL.[1] In August, 1925, Giraud consecrated H. R. GEYER.[2] On August 24th, 1930, Vigné consecrated GUSTAVUS ADOLPHUS GLINZ who, the following day, assisted Vigné to consecrate

FRIEDRICH HEILER[3] as Bishop of the 'Communio Evangelica Catholica Eucharistica'. Later in the same year Giraud consecrated

G. HAUGG. On January 23rd, 1933, Blanchard consecrated CHARLES HORVATH. In October, 1940, Heiler consecrated M. GIEBNER.

III

JOSEPH RENÉ VILATTE, on December 29th, 1915, consecrated FREDERICK EBENEZER JOHN LLOYD[4] as 'Bishop of Illinois'. In 1921 Lloyd consecrated

CARL NYBLADH[5] for the Swedish department of the American Catholic Church. On July 1st, 1923, Lloyd consecrated

GREGORY LINES[6] as 'Bishop of the Pacific'. On June 24th, 1924, Lloyd consecrated

[1] Originally one of Vernon Herford's priests (see pp. 53ff.). Now resident in Austria and calling himself 'Mar Timotheos, Orthodox Missionsbischof'.

[2] He worked in Germany and later consecrated a certain Eugen Herzog.

[3] Dr. Heiler is a widely respected author and scholar. He is said to have a number of adherents in this fellowship who, accepting ordination at his hands, continue to work as pastors of Lutheran parishes.

It is possible that certain of the obscure Gnostic sects in France, which claim to possess an episcopate, received it from one or other of the bishops of this succession. A certain ' Tau Harmonius ' of the ' Gnostic Church ' claimed to have been consecrated by Vilatte. A full account of these sects will be found in two books by Pierre Geyraud, *Les petites Eglises de Paris* and *Les Religions nouvelles de Paris*. It is quite clear, from the descriptions of the rites of consecration of Gnostic bishops which Geyraud gives, that if they ever possessed valid Orders, the rites they use are not of a kind which could transmit them.

[4] Lloyd had been degraded from the Anglican priesthood on January 16th, 1907, by the Bishop of Pittsburgh, and in February of the same year he joined the Church of Rome. In 1909 he again became an Anglican, and nothing more is known of him until his consecration. He succeeded Vilatte as Primate in 1920; he retired early in 1932, and died a year later.

[5] Formerly a priest of the Protestant Episcopal Church in charge of a purely Swedish congregation in Chicago. He tried to take his parish with him when he was consecrated and did succeed in detaching most of the people, but his work did not last, and the parish is flourishing again within the Episcopal Church.

[6] Lines was a priest of the Protestant Episcopal Church, deposed on June 4th, 1894. He twice went into schism from the Lloyd body (see Table IV).

AXEL ZACHARIAS FRYXELL[1] to continue Nybladh's Swedish work. On September 16th, 1926, Fryxell consecrated

CASIMIR FRANCOIS DURAND. In 1926 Lloyd secretly consecrated

FRANCIS KANSKI.[2] On March 27th, 1927, Lloyd consecrated

DANIEL CASSEL HINTON[3] as his Bishop-Auxiliary. On Easter Day, 1927, Fryxell consecrated

ARTHUR EDWARD LEIGHTON.[4] On June 1st, 1927, Lloyd consecrated

ERNEST LEOPOLD PETERSON.[5] In 1927-28 Lines went into schism from the Lloyd Church, and during this time consecrated

JUSTIN A. BOYLE.[6] In 1929 Boyle consecrated

LOWELL PAUL WADLE.[7] On February 2nd, 1930, Lloyd consecrated

FRANCIS IGNATIUS BORYZSEWSKI.[8] In 1930 Fryzell consecrated

WILLIAM O. HOMER.[9] In August, 1933, Hinton consecrated

[1] Formerly a priest of the Protestant Episcopal Church and deposed, upon renunciation of Orders, by the Bishop of Massachusetts on May 4th, 1894. In 1921 he received the Minor Orders, subdiaconate and diaconate from Lloyd and the priesthood from Nybladh. He died in 1934.

[2] Lloyd confessed to this action the following year, and in 1928 the American Catholic Church accepted Kanski. He is at present partially paralysed and comparatively inactive, though still ordaining and consecrating.

[3] Hinton became Primate of the American Catholic Church on Lloyd's retirement. Throughout his career he has been quite free of the graver irregularities of episcopal vagrancy, and is now reconciled with the Protestant Episcopal Church.

[4] He later broke with Fryxell and travelled on his own, leaving a mixed trail of "Old Catholicism" and Spiritism. He has been inactive for a number of years.

[5] A negro and compiler of their liturgy.

[6] Formerly a Roman Catholic priest. He is now inactive ecclesiastically, and operates some kind of service of advice for that part of the public which will pay for advice about life's problems.

[7] A member of the Theosophical Society. He continued as independent until 1940, when Clarkson (see below) received him and made him co-adjutor. On Clarkson's death Wadle assumed the title of Archbishop. So far as is known he has only one parish, though he describes himself as 'Primate of the American Catholic (Vilatte Succession) Apostolic Church of Long Beach'. He has consecrated a certain Michael Strange.

[8] Formerly one of Carfora's priests; he functioned in New York.

[9] Formerly a priest of the Protestant Episcopal Church. He was twice divorced before his consecration, and is now inactive.

PERCY WISE CLARKSON[1].

On December 16th, 1933, Lines consecrated

HOWARD E. MATHER[2] (known as Timothy Mather). On May 1st, 1934, Kanski consecrated

DENVER SCOTT SWAIN.[3]

IV

JOSEPH RENÉ VILATTE, on September 28th, 1921, con secrated a negro from Antigua

GEORGE ALEXANDER McGUIRE[4] as first bishop of the 'African Orthodox Church' which was organised by negro Churchmen in September, 1921.[5] On November 18th, 1923, Lloyd consecrated for this body

WILLIAM ERNEST ROBERTSON,[6] who, in September, 1924, assisted McGuire to consecrate

ARTHUR STANLEY TROTMAN. On September 11th, 1927, McGuire consecrated

DANIEL WILLIAM ALEXANDER[7] to be 'Primate of the Province of South Africa.' On February 12th, 1928, McGuire consecrated

WILLIAM F. TYARCHS[8] as 'first bishop of the American Catholic Orthodox Church.' Later in the same year Tyarchs consecrated

[1] Formerly a priest of the Protestant Episcopal Church, and later a Liberal Catholic. He was consecrated because, owing to Lines' second schism, he was isolated on the Pacific Coast with no bishop to serve his people unless Hinton travelled from Chicago. He had a cathedral in Los Angeles, in which the teaching included numerology and other strange superstitions. He died in 1940.

[2] This consecration was performed during Lines' second schism from the American Catholic Church, caused by his annoyance that Hinton, rather than himself, was designated Primate. Mather is a Congregational minister, though he was received into Lloyd's Order of Antioch, in 1925 or 1926. Subsequently he was made a deacon by Tyarchs of the African Orthodox Church and a priest by Leighton of the succession from Fryxell. Mather now calls himself 'Archbishop and Exarch of the Order of Antioch'.

[3] Very thorough exposures of Swain were published in *The Chicago Sun* of January 4th and 5th, 1945.

[4] McGuire was elected Primate of the body in 1924, and took the title of Patriarch; he is now dead.

[5] See *Apostolic Succession of the African Orthodox Church*, p. 4.

[6] Succeeded McGuire as Primate, and by various actions provoked a schism in the African Orthodox Church which still obtains.

[7] Alexander resides in the Anglican diocese of Kimberley and Kuruman; his actual following anywhere is not large, and there appear to be various schisms in his body.

[8] Deposed by McGuire in 1932. In March, 1945, he was arrested for organizing fraudulent charities, and is now in prison.

CLEMENT C. J. SHERWOOD.[1] On May 30th, 1930, McGuire consecrated

ROBERT ARTHUR VALENTINE.[2] Robertson, some time prior to May, 1940, consecrated

RICHARD GRANT ROBINSON.

V

FREDERICK E. J. LLOYD, on September 8th, 1929, consecrated

CHURCHILL SIBLEY[3] as 'Missionary Archbishop and Vicar-General of the Order of Antioch in England'. On March 8th, 1935, Sibley consecrated

EBENEZER JOHNSON ANDERSON[4] (otherwise known as 'Mar Kwamin Ntsetse Bresi-Ando') as Primate of the 'Autonomous African Universal Church and other unifications of West African Churches in Africa and Florida of the Orthodox Faith'. On September 1st, 1935, Anderson consecrated

FREDERICK CHARLES ALOYSIUS HARRINGTON[5] (otherwise known as 'Mar Frederic') as Primate of the 'Orthodox Keltic Church of the British Commonwealth of Nations'. Sibley, on October 6th, 1935, consecrated

JOHN SEBASTIEN MARLOW WARD[6] of the Abbey of Christ the King, New Barnet. On November 16th, 1935, Harrington consecrated

[1] At one time a subordinate of Brothers; he was re-consecrated by McGuire after Tyarchs had fallen into disgrace.

[2] He is now head of the larger, and more reputable, of the two factions into which the African Orthodox Church is split.

[3] Sibley resided in England, his main occupation being that of English representative of the Intercollegiate University, an institution whose degrees are not generally recognized as conferring academic distinction. He died in 1939.

[4] He resided in London for some years, but has now returned to the Gold Coast. The following claim for his organization was made in *The Hornsey Journal* of September 13th, 1935: "This Church is in full communion with the Abyssinian and Coptic Churches . . . while in South America there are two Provinces under the guidance of the same Primate." This claim is to be treated as seriously as that made elsewhere in the same article that "The Orthodox Catholic Church in Africa, which is led by the Primate, consists of considerably over 20 million people". He now calls himself 'Prince-Patriarch of Apam'.

[5] Harrington attempted to unite all the Vilatte and Ferrete bodies under himself, and for this purpose was re-consecrated in 1938 by Heard of the Ferrete succession. He made fantastic claims as to the number of his adherents, but his actual following was negligible. Towards the end of his life he abandoned ecclesiastical work and was employed by the London County Council. He died in 1942.

[6] Ward is an authority on the esoteric side of Freemasonry, and a list of his publications on the subject will be found in *Who's Who*; he is

JAMES DOMINIC MARY O'GAVIGAN.[1] On October 24th, 1937, Harrington consecrated

DORIAN HERBERT[2] as 'Bishop of Caerleon'. On May 28th, 1940, O'Gavigan consecrated

GEORGE HENRY BROOK,[3] otherwise known as 'Mar Adrianus, Bishop of Deira'. Herbert, on August 1st, 1943, consecrated

FRANCIS DAVID BACON[4] as 'Bishop of Repton'.

---

proprietor of a 'Folk Park' and head of a small mixed community which at one time accepted the jurisdiction of the Bishop of St. Albans, and attained some notoriety in 1945 on account of a law-suit. He has entered into some sort of federation with Newman of the Ferrete succession and is known as 'John, Archbishop of Olivet'.

[1] O'Gavigan later parted from Harrington and joined the American Catholic Church (Lloyd), and from them received authorization to set up an independent branch of that body in England. He operated in the West of England, and was killed during an air-raid. He had been re-consecrated in the Mathew, Vilatte and Ferrete lines of succession, and made the curious claim that they all 'met' in his person.

[2] Herbert resides at Abergavenny, and is head of a small body variously styled the 'Jesuene Church' and the 'Free Orthodox-Catholic Church'. In a leaflet entitled *The Jesuene Church*, Herbert says: "The Jesuene Church is rationalistic in its interpretation, unorthodox and heretical. We base the unity of our organization upon the acceptance, as a true standard of human conduct, of the moral code and precepts laid down in the life and teaching of Jesus recorded in the Four Gospels. We do not profess any creed, nor do we regard 'belief' as a criterion of membership of the Church." In December, 1944, Herbert received conditional re-consecration from Newman of the Ferrete succession.

[3] Brook was re-consecrated by Newman in December, 1944.

[4] See a leaflet, *Consecration of a Bishop*, reprinted from *The Abergavenny Chronicle*, which describes Bacon as 'Bishop of Mercia, which is something of a courtesy title'. Bacon is the author of a small handbook on the Eastern Churches entitled *An Eastern Pilgrimage*. He was re-consecrated by Newman in 1946.

CHAPTER V

THE FERRETE SUCCESSION

JULIUS FERRETE was professed in 1850 as a Dominican under the name of Brother Raymond, and was ordained priest by Cardinal Patrizi in the Church of St. John Lateran. In 1860 he is said to have developed opinions concerning the divisions of Christendom which were inconsistent with his office as a Roman Catholic priest. Nothing further is known of his history until the year 1866, when he arrived in England claiming to have been consecrated as "Bishop of Iona" by Mgr. Bedros, Bishop of Emesa (Homs) of the Syrian Antiochene Church and later Patriarch of Antioch under the title of Ignatius Peter III. Ferrete produced no evidence of this consecration beyond a printed document which purported to be a translation of his certificate of consecration, at the bottom of which the name of the British Consul at Damascus is printed in testimony. The date of this is June 2nd, 1866 (Old Style). It is obvious that, while this printed document may have been a perfectly genuine translation of the original certificate of consecration, it is in itself quite worthless as evidence, and no more convincing proof of the genuineness of Ferrete's claim has ever been produced. Dr. Pusey, who went to some trouble to investigate the claim at the time, stated that: "There seems to me a *prima facie* improbability that he was consecrated Bishop of Iona".[1] Malcolm MacColl, who also investigated Ferrete's claims very thoroughly, contended that he was an "impudent adventurer" and declared: "Whether the 'Bishop of Iona' went through any form of conferring episcopal consecration on anyone I know not; but I do know that he had no orders of his own to bestow".[2]

However this may be, Ferrete came to England in the summer of 1866, and in September of that year he published in London *The Eastern Liturgy adapted for Use in the West.* In the "Pastoral Letter" affixed to this book, Ferrete declared himself ready "to give Holy Orders to pious and learned men, who, being duly elected, will declare themselves willing to conform to this Liturgy". The response was

[1] Manuscript letter. [2] *The Times*, September 13th, 1898.

apparently very slight and, owing to the attacks upon him, Ferrete withdrew his offer, and departed from England in 1874 after consecrating a successor named Morgan, and died in Switzerland.

The succession from Ferrete early became involved with that of the 'Free Protestant Church of England', a body which still has some shadowy existence.[1] The connecting link was the somewhat dubious Armenian prelate, Leon Chechemian, who had been elected Archbishop of the Free Protestant Church of England in 1897, "and as such consecrated by six bishops". Chechemian was re-consecrated by Morgan, thus apparently undergoing three consecrations.[2] McLaglen and Maaers, the two bishops who succeeded Chechemian, both seem to have reverted to some form of Protestantism, but McLaglen, by the consecration of Heard in 1922, sought to secure the continuance of the original Ferrete line. For a number of years the succession remained more or less dormant, and no further consecrations were performed, apart from the consecration of Hayman, in 1930, for the so-called 'Free Catholic Church'. In recent years, however, the succession has blossomed into a new life with a number of consecrations of bishops and very considerable paper pretensions.

The guiding spirit of this revival in its early stages was probably Harrington of the Vilatte succession, who was re-consecrated by Heard in 1938 with the intention of uniting under himself the Vilatte and Ferrete successions in England. Little further progress appears to have been made during Harrington's lifetime, perhaps owing to his obvious unsuitability and his financial embarrassments. Harrington has been succeeded, however, by H. G. de Willmott Newman, who describes himself as 'Catholicos of the West and Patriarch of Glastonbury'.

This revival bases its claims on the assertion that by the consecration of Ferrete in 1866 the Metran of Homs gave authority for the setting up of autokephalous Syrian Churches in the West. Another version of the claim is that the authority was given by this same Metran, after he had become the Patriarch Ignatius Peter III, in the Bull authorizing the consecration of Vilatte. It may be mentioned in passing that nothing was heard of this supposed authority for the creation of autokephalous churches in the West until 1943, nearly eighty years after it is supposed to have been given. The claims will not stand the test of investigation.

[1] See p. 52.

[2] See p. 50.

In the first place, the Metran of Homs does not himself possess authority to authorize the setting-up of autokephalous churches and, indeed, there is no evidence whatever that he attempted to do so. In the second place, there is not a word, in any of the supposed translations of the Bull, authorizing the consecration of Vilatte which lends colour to such a supposition, and in them Vilatte is spoken of as subject to the Antiochene See. The story of the present development is best told in the words of a leaflet issued by the body in question:[1]

"In 1943 a division took place among the Jacobites, those who adhered to Monophysitism continuing as the Syrian Orthodox Church under the Patriarch Ignatius Ephrem I, whilst another section at the Council of London repudiated Monophysitism and Jansenism and elected as Patriarch of Antioch H. H. Basilius Abdullah III and adopted the title 'The Ancient Orthodox Catholic Church'. This was not a revolt against Ignatius Ephrem I, for he himself in 1938 had severed all connection with certain portions of his Patriarchate,[2] which, being left in a position analogous to that visualized by Canons 37 and 39 of the Council of Trullo, A.D. 691,[3] had no alternative but to elect a Patriarch, and at

[1] *Catholicate of the West: Historical Notes concerning the Western Orthodox Catholic Church.* Orthodox Catholic Leaflets, No. 2.

[2] See Appendix A; no Patriarch of Antioch, of course, had ever regarded these schisms as part of the Patriarchate.

[3] The Canons are as follows; it will be seen how little they in fact apply to the present situation:

Canon xxxvii: "Quoniam diversis temporibus barbaricae incursiones fuere, et ex eo plurimae civitates infidelibus subjugatae fuere, ut ideo non posuit ejus civitatis praesul postquam ordinatus fuerit, suum thronum apprehendere, et in eo in sacerdotali constitutione collocari, et sic pro ea quae invaluit consuetudine ordinationes et omnia, quae ad episcopum pertirent, agere et tractare: nos honorem ac venerationem sacerdotio servantes, et Gentilem injuriam nequaquam ad ecclesiasticorum jurium perniciem exerceri volentes; eos qui sic ordinati sunt, et propter praedictam sausam in suis thronis non sunt constituti, ut obsque ullo ex ea re praejudicio conserventur, decrevimus: ut et diversorum clericorum ordinationes canonice faciant, et praesedentiae auctoritate secundum proprium statum utantur, et sit firma ac legitima quaecumque ab eis procedit administratio. Non enim a tempore necessitatis exacta juris observatione circumscripta, dispensationis terminus circumscribetur."

Canon xxxix: "Cum frater et comminister noster Ioannis insulae Cypri praesul, una cum suo populo in Hellesponticam provinciam et propter barbaricas incursiones, et ut Gentilium servitute liberarentur, et Christianissimae potentiae sceptris pure subjucerentur, et praedicta insula emigraverit, clemtis Dei providentia et pii Deique amantis imperatoris nostri labore, constituimus, ut citra ullam innovationem

the same time took the opportunity of making their formal submission to the Seven Œcumenical Councils.

"By a deed of Declaration dated 23rd of March, 1944, the Ancient British Church, the Independent Catholic Church, and the British Orthodox Catholic Church, all previously referred to, united with the Old Catholic Orthodox Church. This latter body was derived from the Old Catholic Movement established in Britain in 1908 by the late Archbishop Arnold Harris Mathew,[1] who had been received into union with the Greek Orthodox Patriarchs of Antioch and Alexandria in 1911 and 1912 respectively. The united Church adopted the title 'The Western Orthodox Catholic Church', and was constituted as the Catholicate of the West by the Patriarch Basilius Abdullah III and thereupon became a fully autonomous and autocephalous member of the family of Orthodox Churches with full territorial jurisdiction in Britain and Western Europe."

The so-called 'Patriarch Basilius Abdullah III' claims, however, not merely to be Patriarch of the small groups in the West which claim descent from the Antiochene Patriarchate, but he claims actually to be Patriarch of Antioch in the place of Mar Ignatius Ephrem I. In a leaflet issued by him the following account is given of the 'Council of London':

"In 1943 Mar James (Heard), the senior Bishop of these groups derived from the Patriarchate of Antioch, convened the Council of London . . . The acts of this Council are summarized as follows:

(i) The Council, embracing steadfastly the definitions of the Seven Œcumenical Councils and the Holy Apostolic

serventur, quae a divinis patribus, qui Ephesi primum convererunt, praedicti viri throno privilegia concessa sunt, it nova Iustinianopolis Constantinopoleas jus habeat, et qui in ea constituitur pius ac religiossimus episcopus, praesit omnibus Hellespontiorum provinciae episcopis, et a suis episcopis eligatur ex antiqua consuetudine. Mores enim, qui sunt in unaquaque ecclesia, divini etiam nostri patres servandos censuerunt, Cyzicenorum civitatis episcopo praesuli dictae Iustinianopoleas subjecto existente, ad imitationem reliquorum omnium episcoporum, qui subsunt praedicto Dei amantissimo preasuli Ioanni; et quo cum usus postulaverit, etiam ipsius Cyzicenorum civitatis episcopus ordinabitur."

[1] i.e. through Banks who had been consecrated by Willoughby, but there was no connection with Mathew's own movement, and this statement has since been amended to read: "The Old Catholic Orthodox Church; a Body of Old Catholics which came into separate existence in 1925, and based its position upon the Declaration of Utrecht, 1889, and accepted the dogmatic decrees of the Holy Synod of Jerusalem, 1672, held by the Greek Orthodox Church."

Traditions, repudiated the heresies of Monophysitism and Jansenism and all other heresies; (ii) that in view of Ignatius Ephrem I having disclaimed all connection with the above mentioned extensions of his Patriarchate, lawfully made by his predecessor, the said Ignatius Ephrem was no longer recognized as holding office, that in consequence of the Patriarchal Synod and many of the Bishops in Syria and Malabar having adhered to the aforementioned, the right to elect to the vacant see was declared to be now vested in the Council; (iii) that in order to prevent confusion with the followers of the adherents of the aforementioned Patriarch it was provided that the Church within the rightful Patriarchate of Antioch should no longer be called 'the Syrian Orthodox' or 'Jacobite' Church, but should be hereafter known as 'the Ancient Orthodox Catholic Church' and by no other name; that the original jurisdiction of the Patriarchate should remain as heretofore, but its extensions in the West were specifically recognized and confirmed in their rights; that the traditional name 'Ignatius' in the official designation of the Patriarch should be abandoned, and the name 'Basilius' substituted therefor; that the full patriarchal title should in future be as follows: 'His Holiness Mohoran Mar Basilius *N*, Sovereign Prince Patriarch of the God-protected City of Antioch and of all the domain of the Apostolic Throne, both in the East and in the West; (iv) Mar Bernard,[1] Bishop of St. Sophia (Grand Master of the Order of the Holy Wisdom) was elected to the vacant Patriarchal See of Antioch under the title Basilius Abdullah III, to whom all bishops dependent upon the See of Antioch were required to make their canonical submission within six months from the date of the Council, unless lawfully hindered."[2]

This farrago of nonsense carries its own condemnation. So far as can be ascertained, no one prelate who had ever been in communion with the See of Antioch took part in this "election", which was conducted in a manner not in accordance with the Canons of that Church by a group of Englishmen whose connection with the Antiochene Patriarchate is, to say the least, a matter of dispute.

[1] William Bernard Crow.

[2] *Patriarchate of Antioch: Ancient Orthodox Catholic Church*, pp. 3–4.

The Ferrete Succession

I

Julius Ferrete consecrated, at Marholm, Northamptonshire, in 1874,

Richard Williams Morgan,[1] curate of that place, as 'Archbishop of Caerleon-on-Usk'. In 1879 Morgan, assisted by F. G. Lee and J. T. Seccombe (see p. 64) consecrated,

Charles Isaac Stevens, who, in 1890, assisted by Bishop A. S. Richardson,[2] formerly of the Reformed Episcopal Church, consecrated *sub conditione*,

Leon Chechemian,[3] who, on November 2nd, 1897, consecrated

Andrew Charles Albert McLagen as 'Colonial Missionary Bishop and Titular Bishop of Claremont' and

G. W. L. Maaers.[4] On June 4th, 1922, McLaglen consecrated

James Heard as 'Archbishop of Selsey', who, on June 13th, 1943, consecrated

William Bernard Crow[5] who, on April 10th, 1944, consecrated

[1] Morgan is stated to have been a fanatic obsessed with the vision of a British Church which should restore the doctrine and discipline of the days before St. Augustine. For the earlier part of this succession see *A Chapter of Secret History*, reprinted from *The Church Times* of April 28th, 1922, with notes by F. E. Langhelt.

[2] Richardson had been consecrated in the Reformed Episcopal Church in Philadelphia in 1879, and he later resided in England. He was adjudicated bankrupt by the Courts and, in accordance with the Canons of the Reformed Episcopal Church, resigned his jurisdiction in it. He later seceded from the body, and was concerned in various doubtful episcopal enterprises. He died at Boulogne in 1907.

[3] Leon Chechemian is said to have been Armenian Uniate titular Bishop of Malatia. He became a Protestant, and published a tract *An Eastern's Steps from Darkness to Light.* He was known to Bishop Temple of London, and in 1890 Lord Plunket, Archbishop of Dublin, granted him a licence in his diocese. His re-consecration was apparently due to the fact that as an Armenian titular bishop he had no jurisdiction to perform consecrations, but it is not clear how conditional re-consecration might be supposed to confer it upon him.

[4] The date here given for Maaers' consecration is that given in Harrington's pamphlet of his episcopal succession, as well as in *A Chapter of Secret History*. It does not, however, tally with a contemporary newspaper account of McLaglen's consecration, where Maaers is given as one of the consecrators—*Star*, December 21st, 1897.

[5] Crow now describes himself as 'His Holiness Mohoran Mar Basilius Abdullah III, Sovereign Prince Patriarch of Antioch'. He was formerly a Theosophist attached as priest to the Liberal Catholic Church, and

HUGH GEORGE DE WILLMOTT NEWMAN[1] (otherwise known as 'Mar Georgius I) as 'Archbishop and Metropolitan of Glastonbury and Catholicos of the West'. Newman, on May 20th, 1945, consecrated

WILLIAM JOHN EATON JEFFREY[2] as 'Bishop of St. Marylebone.' On April 22nd, 1946, Newman consecrated

RICHARD KENNETH HURGON as 'Benignus, Titular Bishop of Mere'. On June 6th, 1946, Newman consecrated

WALLACE DAVID DE ORTEGA MAXEY [3] and COLIN MACKENZIE CHAMBERLAIN.[4]

Heard also consecrated, on Easter Monday, 1930,

VICTOR ALEXANDER PALMER HAYMAN[5] as 'Bishop of Wal-

---

is by profession a lecturer in biology (See his biography in *Who's Who*). Crow's main interest appears to be as that of 'Grand Master of the Order of the Holy Wisdom', which is thus described in one of its leaflets: "Being absolutely universal (that is truly Orthodox and Catholic), it has access to the divine wisdom or Theosophy embodied in the symbols of all nations. It utilizes the knowledge passed on in the great streams of sacred tradition, not excluding those of the so-called Primitive Religions, those of the Far East, the Brahmanic-Yogic, Ancient Egyptian, Zoroastrian-Magian, Kabalistic, Gnostic-Masonic, Gothic-Rosicrucian, Druidic-Bacchic, Chaldean, Buddhist-Lamaistic and Islamic-Sufic . . . The Order has for its special object the establishment and maintenance of a planetary and zodiacal temple of the universal religion, the preparation and initiation of suitable candidates, and the celebration of the ancient Mysteries in their pristine form." It will probably be held that nonsense of this kind renders Crow's sacramental ministrations of doubtful validity on the grounds of intention.

[1] For Newman see the account of him in *The Year Book of the Incorporated Institute of Cycle Traders and Repairers*, 1944. He was ordained priest by McFall of the Mathew succession, and was at one time associated with Brooks of the 'Chaldean Succession' (see pp. 67–68), at which time he described himself as 'Titular Abbot of St. Alban'. He is not now in communion with Crow, but he claims to have received into union with himself a number of other *episcopi vagantes*, to whom he has given conditional re-consecration, and then himself received consecration from them with a view to "combining the lines of succession" under the apparent misconception that a person is consecrated a bishop of a particular line of succession rather than a bishop of the Church of God. (See *The Orthodox Catholic Review* for May, 1945, and Newman's *Pastoral Letter for Advent 1945*.)

[2] Jeffery was trustee of Herford's 'Evangelical Catholic Communion, and was consecrated to succeed Bartlett (see p. 55). He is at present minister of the King's Weigh House.

[3] Maxey was invested with the title of 'His Beatitude Mar David I., Patriarch of Malaga, Apostolic Primate of all the Iberians, and Supreme Hierarch of the Catholicate of the West in the Americas'.

[4] One of Ward's men at the Abbey of Christ the King, see p. 43.

[5] Formerly an Anglican priest in the Diocese of Chelmsford. Hayman was later connected with Sir Oswald Mosley's movement, and, having been inactive for a number of years, appears now to be working with Newman.

thamstow' of the 'Free Catholic Church', while Heard also, on May 18th, 1939, consecrated

WILLIAM HALL as 'Bishop of Middlesex and the Eastern Counties' of the 'Free Protestant Church'. On November 28th, 1946, Newman consecrated

HERMAN PHILIPPUS ABBINGA.[1]

THE FERRETE SUCCESSION

II

LEON CHECHEMIAN in 1890, consecrated,

JAMES MARTIN as 'Archbishop and Patriarch' of the 'Free Protestant Church of England'.[2] Martin, in 1917, consecrated

BENJAMIN CHARLES HARRIS as 'Bishop of Essex'. On November 17th, 1944, Harris consecrated

CHARLES LESLIE SAUL,

JAMES CHARLES RYAN[3] and

GORDON PINDER, 'Archbishop of Preston'.[4]

[1] Formerly a Liberal Catholic priest, who had been ordained up to, and including, the priesthood *sub conditione* by Maxey, and consecrated on October 13th, 1946, by Arthur Wolfort Brooks (see p. 67). Abbinga is now described as 'Mar Philippus, Bishop of Amersfoort, and Vicar-Apostolic of the Catholicate of the West in the Netherlands and Dutch East Indies'.

[2] Not to be confused with the 'Free Church of England, otherwise called the Reformed Episcopal Church', which is an offshoot of the Cumminsite schism in America. An account of the sect, which appears to have had a very tenuous existence, is given in *The Origin, Orders, Organization, etc., of the Free Protestant Episcopal Church of England* by Ernest A. Asquith (1917). There was also an Ernest Mumby at one time a bishop of the body.

[3] Saul and Ryan have now placed themselves under Newman's jurisdiction, where they have taken the titles respectively of 'Leofric, Archbishop of Suthronia' and 'James, Archbishop of India'. Ryan's real name is Chengalraryan Chittoor Pitlai. He was originally converted to Christianity by an offshoot of the Methodist Episcopal Church, and later was ordained 'bishop' of the body by the laying-on of hands of the presbytery. The body later adopted the name of 'Evangelical Church in India', and its mission was said to be to the untouchables. He has for a number of years appeared in various parts of England, preaching in Nonconformist chapels. Saul has recently ordained various priests.

[4] Pinder heads the 'Northern Province of the Evangelical Church of England', which Province has not entered into union with Newman. This is some kind of Protestant body and Pinder claimed in a newspaper interview that it "existed to open parishes in districts without churches and also where the local parish church had become Anglo-Catholic". They seem to use the Prayer Book of 1662.

CHAPTER VI

BISHOP VERNON HERFORD

THE consecration of Ulric Vernon Herford is alleged to have taken place on St. Andrew's Day, 1902, at Palithamam, near Kaliarkoil, Madura District, South India. Herford himself gave the following account of it:

"My consecration came about thus. Our group of Christians desired to be in the Catholic Church in an orderly and regular way without violating our consciences. We could subscribe to the real Nicene Creed (We believe in one God . . . and in the Holy Spirit. Amen. Still the official Creed of the East Syrians), and the only Œcumenical Creed. . . . Mar Basilius, representing the reasonable tradition of the school of Antioch, was able and willing to help us. So, in the regular way, not with a *congé d'élire*, but with a petition from our people, I went to him, and was ordained and consecrated on the basis of this Creed."[1]

Concerning this Mar Basilius Herford wrote as follows:

"Luis Mariano Soares (or Suares) Mar Basilius, was a Roman Catholic cleric of Goa, of Brahmin descent. He was ordained priest by Mar Julius (Alvares), of the 'Independent Catholics' of Ceylon,[2] who was consecrated by the (majority) Jacobite 'Thomas Christians'. Mgr. Soares was then elected by a body of Indian Christians in the Madura district—who had revolted from the hard and exacting rule of the Jesuit Mission—to preside over them, and was consecrated by Mar Abd-Tshu, who, in the words of the late Mar Benjamin Shimun, *de jure* Patriarch of the historic Catholic Church of India (East Syrian or Syro-Chaldean) 'had full power and authority by the consecration which he received from the Patriarch, to bind and to loose, and to ordain and consecrate bishops and priests and other clergy as he might find necessary for the work of the Church."

Considerable confusion exists as to the precise status of Herford's consecrators. Inquiries made in India have failed to produce any adequate evidence of the genuineness

[1] *The Guardian*, October 13th, 1922. [2] See pp. 33–34.

of Mar Abd-Tshu,[1] and in any case Mar Basilius Soares seems to have been recognized as bishop only by a very small sect, which has now disappeared, leaving little trace. There does, however, exist a document in Syriac and English which purports to be the Letters of Consecration of Mar Basilius. In this it is stated:

"On the twenty-third of Tammuz 1899 of the Christian Era, in the great Chaldean Church of the Cathedral City of Trichur, in the presence of the priests and deacons and the Christian people, with our assistant in ordination our honourable Mar Agostinos, Bishop of Trichur, we changed the name of the priest Soares and we called him Basilios. We have instructed him and raised him to the degree of the Metropolitanate for the See of India, Ceylon, Myalpur, Socotra, Messina, etc.

"Given in the cell of our Metropolitanate in Trichur, in Malabar, India, the twenty-fourth of the month Tammuz, in the year 1899 A.D. Mar Abhdisho, by grace (of God) Metropolitan of Malabar."

The Syriac portion of this document was submitted some years ago to experts at the British Museum, whose verdict was that, while it was written by someone with a good knowledge of Syriac, yet the style was far from impeccable and there were a number of faults in grammar and construction. There is no means of testing whether the document is genuine. The only evidence that Herford was able himself to produce in later years in support of his claims was three documents printed in English and sealed with an English rubber stamp. He admitted that the words in the blank spaces in these documents had been written by himself, and he admitted signing Mar Basilius' name to two of

[1] There is some account of him in *Christianity in Travancore*, by G. T. MACKENZIE, from which the following emerges: "About 1850 many of the St. Thomas Christians who were ruled by Roman Catholic bishops, wanted to secure an Eastern bishop and selected the Thondanatta Antony. . . . with twelve years studying for the priesthood two priests and three clerics, in 1858, he set sail for the Persian Gulf. Several died on the journey, but Antony and the survivors returned in 1861 bringing with them a Chaldean bishop named Roccos or Mar Thomas as Metran (Metropolitan), who later submitted to Rome and sailed from Cochin in 1862. Antony went a second time to the Persian Gulf . . . and applied to the Chaldean Patriarch for consecration. The Patriarch, in face of the instructions . . . from Rome dared not himself consecrate Antony, but sent him to the Nestorian Patriarch of Babylon, who consecrated Antony as Bishop. Taking the name of Mar Abedjesus (Abd-Tshu) . . . Antony then returned to India. . . . he died in Trichur on the 16th of November, 1900."

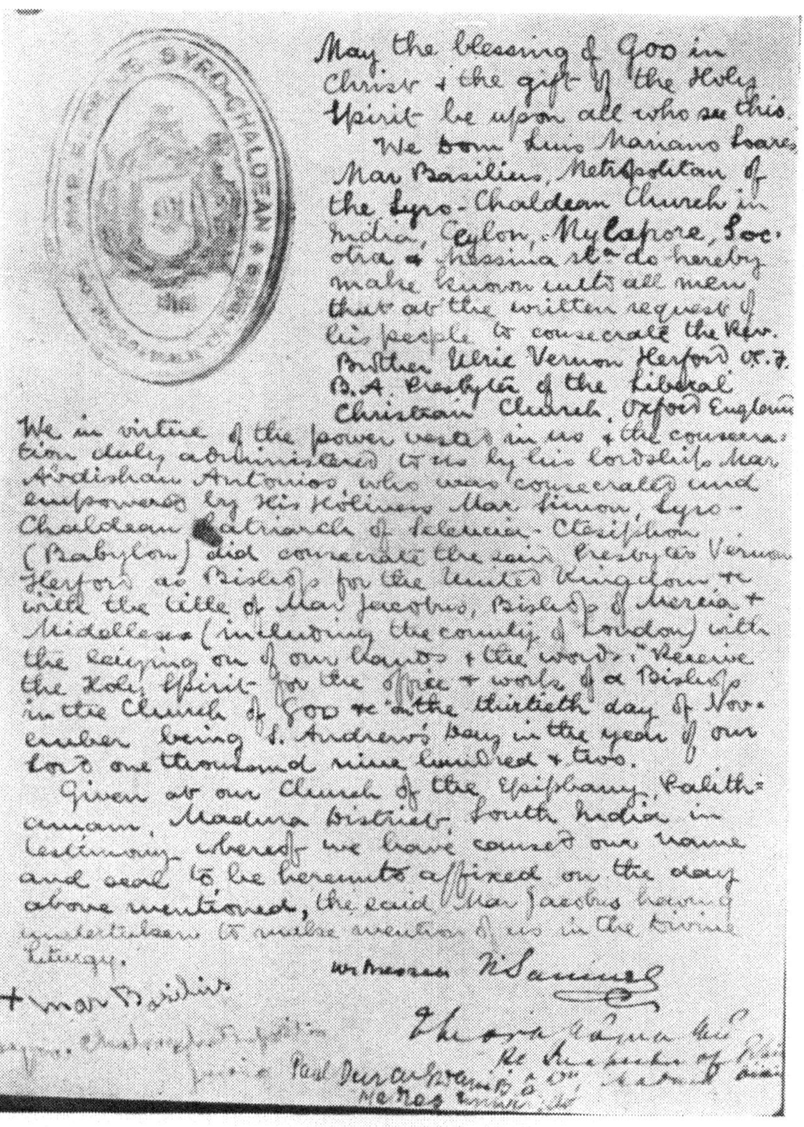

SYRO-CHALDEAN

May the blessing of God in Christ & the gift of the Holy Spirit be upon all who see this.

We Dom Luis Mariano Soares, Mar Basilius, Metropolitan of the Syro-Chaldean Church in India, Ceylon, Mylapore, Socotra & Messina &c do hereby make known unto all men that at the written request of his people to consecrate the Rev. Brother Ulric Vernon Herford O.F. B.A. Presbyter of the Liberal Christian Church, Oxford England We in virtue of the power vested in us & the consecration duly administered to us by his Lordship Mar Ardishar Antonios, who was consecrated and empowered by His Holiness Mar Simon, Syro-Chaldean Patriarch of Seleucia-Ctesiphon (Babylon) did consecrate the said Presbyter Vernon Herford as Bishop for the United Kingdom &c with the title of Mar Jacobus, Bishop of Mercia & Middlesex (including the county of London) with the laying on of our hands & the words "Receive the Holy Spirit for the office & work of a Bishop in the Church of God &c" on the thirtieth day of November being S. Andrew's Day in the year of our Lord one thousand nine hundred & two.

Given at our Church of the Epiphany, Palithanam, Madura District, South India in testimony whereof we have caused our name and seal to be hereunto affixed on the day above mentioned, the said Mar Jacobus having undertaken to make mention of us in the Divine Liturgy.

Witnesses N. Samuel

+ Mar Basilius

Syro-Chaldean Metropolitan

Paul Desa

Thomas Payne

Rt. Inspector of Police

ALLEGED INSTRUMENT OF CONSECRATION OF ULRIC VERNON HERFORD

[*To face p.* 54.

them. He appears to have been unable to account for the fact that the forms of ordination and consecration bear striking resemblance to those in the Anglican Book of Common Prayer, which one would not suppose would be well known to a Brahmin Nestorian in Southern India. These documents are, of course, canonically worthless.

In 1909 the Dutch Old Catholics wrote to Herford declining to recognize the validity of his Orders. De Willmott Newman's organization has recently undertaken an investigation of Herford's claims, and states that "photostat copies of the relevant documents are preserved in the Archives of the Catholicate, and this line of succession must be pronounced to be absolutely valid".[1] Such a verdict certainly could not be pronounced by any competent person upon the evidence of any documents which Herford himself was wont to show. Herford was later re-consecrated by a crypto-bishop called Benedict Donkin.[2]

Herford appears to have had very little following, and it is probable that the 'group of Christians', referred to in his letter to *The Guardian*, consisted of little more than his family and household. Such following as he had he called 'The Evangelical Catholic Communion', and gave himself the title of 'Mercia and Middlesex'. His principal activity appears to have been the clandestine ordination of Free Church ministers who, accepting ordination at his hands, continued to minister in their own communions. These were required to make the following declaration: "I join myself, and all whom I can influence, to the Evangelical Catholic Communion; thus claiming my place within the Catholic tradition without separating myself from my fellow Christians". Some years ago Mr. J. A. Kensit's magazine published the names of a few of the ministers who had received ordination from Herford in this way,[3] but the total number was probably very small.

In the early 1920's Herford consecrated W. S. McBean Knight as 'Archbishop of Kent', who, in August, 1925, consecrated Hedley Coward Bartlett who is described as

[1] *The Orthodox Catholic Review*, May, 1935, p. 39.

[2] Donkin called himself 'Bishop of Santa Croce' and stated consistently, and by affidavit a few hours before his death, that he was consecrated by Sancher y Camachao, a retired Roman Catholic bishop living at El Ovedo, Mexico. He affirmed that the consecration took place at Naples. A trial of Donkin, practically as an impostor, resulted in an acquittal and an opinion from Mr. Justice Grantham that he was a victim of persecution. He has left no succession.

[3] *The Churchman's Magazine*, February, 1922.

'Archbishop of Siluria'. On Whit-Sunday, May 20th, 1945, W. J. E. Jeffery[1] was consecrated to carry on Herford's work. The extraordinary ceremony by which this was performed is described in *The Orthodox Catholic Review*, May 1945:

"On Whit-Sunday, May 20th, five bishops (representing nine independent lines of Apostolic succession) assembled together in the 12th century Chapel of St. John in historic Pembridge Castle, for the purpose of consecrating a Bishop to carry on the work of the Evangelical Catholic Communion founded by the late Bishop Vernon Herford . . . the Consecrators were His Beatitude Mar Georgius, D.D., D.C.L., Archbishop and Metropolitan of Glastonbury and Catholicos of the West; the Rt. Rev. Hedley C. Bartlett, F.S.A., Bishop of Siluria; the Rt. Rev. John Syer, Ph.D., Bishop of Llanthony; the Rt. Rev. F. E. Langhelt, Ph.D., Presiding Bishop of the Old Catholic Church in England and Chancellor to the Catholicate of the West; and the Rt. Rev. Mar Adrianus, Bishop of Deira . . . Prior to the main ceremony, all the five consecrators formally merged their respective orders and successions by means of consecration *sub conditione* so as to form one united line in the interests of Christian Reunion . . . The consecration of Father Jeffery was performed according to the ancient, simple East Syrian Rite. . . ."

[1] See p. 51.

CHAPTER VII

THE AFTIMIOS SUCCESSION

AFTIMIOS OFIESH was originally a monk and priest of the Orthodox Patriarchate of Antioch. He was elected bishop by the Russian Holy Synod and consecrated on May 11th, 1917, by Archbishop Evdokim, who had himself been consecrated by Macarius of Moscow. In 1927, on the initiative of the Metropolitan Platon and, apparently, with the approval of Archbishop Sergius of Moscow, *locum tenens* of the Russian Patriarchate, a group of Orthodox bishops in America sponsored an autokephalous North American Orthodox Church to unite all racial Orthodox Churches in North America. Aftimios was appointed President of the Holy Synod of this organization and Archbishop of Brooklyn. The scheme collapsed when all the autokephalous churches ignored the "Letter of Peace" circulated by Aftimios, and the Œcumenical Patriarch declared that an act of schism had been committed. The Russian bishops withdrew their support, and Aftimios was isolated. In 1933 Aftimios married, and was consequently deposed by a decree signed by the Metropolitan Sergius and promulgated in the United States by the Archbishop-Exarch, Benjamin. Aftimios then desisted from further ecclesiastical acts and retired to Pennsylvania.

Before his marriage Aftimios consecrated two bishops, Joseph A. Zuk and Ignatius W. A. Nichols. From Nichols there exists a somewhat tangled stream of irregular succession.

THE AFTIMIOS SUCCESSION

ARCHBISHOP EVDOKIM, on May 11th, 1917, consecrated
AFTIMIOS OFIESH, who, apparently early in 1932, consecrated
JOSEPH A. ZUK.[1] On September 27th, 1932, Aftimios consecrated

[1] A Ukranian Orthodox priest. He died in 1934, and his following was taken over by Metropolitan Platon.

IGNATIUS WILLIAM ALBERT NICHOLS[1] as 'Bishop of Washington'. In May, 1934, Nichols consecrated

GEORGE WINSLOW PLUMMER.[2] In April or May, 1934, Plummer appears to have re-consecrated three of his former bishops

HARRY VAN ARSDALE PARSELL,

ADRIAN GROVER and

MARCUS ALLEN GROVER. On November 12th, 1939, Nichols consecrated

ALEXANDER TYLER TURNER[3] "Provincial of the Clerks Secular of St. Basil". Early in 1940 Nichols consecrated

FRANK DYER.[4] Early in 1942 Dyer performed some kind of consecration ceremony upon

J. MORRISON THOMAS[5] and

[1] Formerly of the Protestant Episcopal Church, which he left in 1922. Later he was ordained priest by Lines of the Vilatte succession. He was by profession a journalist, and had been religious editor of several New York City newspapers, including the *Sun* and *World Telegram*. He was first consecrated by Leighton, but on discovering his character broke off all connection with him. He is thus described by one who knew him: "When I knew him in 1934 Nichols was a sporty old dog. He wore his clericals in the newspaper office, and when we got on the ferry boat to go to his home on Staten Island, I followed him down the length of the deck, while he greeted everyone he knew cordially with a word and the sign of the cross in blessing. Picturesque is no word for him. He had a dollar up on 'the horses' every afternoon, and in a very warm and human way was very much of the bohemian world of newspaperdom." He died in December, 1946.

[2] Formerly a Roman Catholic priest. Until 1934 he operated as head of the 'Anglican Universal Church', the orders of which, it was claimed, came by the consecration of Plummer by Manuel Ferrando, of Puerto Rico, of the Reformed Episcopal Succession. Ferrando is reported to have denied this consecration. Plummer died in January 1944, and has been succeeded by James R. C. Toombs, who appears to have been consecrated subsequent to Plummer's death.

[3] Formerly pastor of a Liberal Catholic parish in Rochester, N.Y. His organization, the Society of Clerks Secular of St. Basil, has some eight priests and one or two deacons in it. They follow the medieval rule of Hours, while engaged also in earning a livelihood in secular vocations. A note about the organization is in *Time* for September 3rd, 1945.

[4] A well-known Congregational minister. He was ordained priest by Lloyd while serving in the Congregational Church. When Lloyd died he found sanctuary with Gregory Lines and his co-adjutor, Howard E. Mather, at whose request he was consecrated.

[5] This man has for a quarter of a century been Pastor of the Ravenswood Congregational Church of Chicago. He and Bradley were 'consecrated' in the same ceremony. The whole affair was surrounded with secrecy, but it has since developed that Dyer did not perform these ordaining and consecrating ceremonies during the Holy Eucharist, but merely performed some rite of laying-on of hands. The consecrations,

PRESTON BRADLEY.[1]

---

therefore, are almost certainly invalid. Later in the same year Thomas was again consecrated by Mather of the Vilatte succession, and early in 1943, at the instigation of A. T. B. Haines, was consecrated a third time, by Carfora. He is still pastor of the Ravenswood Congregational Church.

[1] A Unitarian who has for a number of years been pastor of the Peoples Church of North Side, Chicago. He is a prominent public speaker and widely known as a radio commentator. Later in 1942 he was re-consecrated by Mather, and is now known as a bishop of the Order of Antioch.

CHAPTER VIII

THE POLISH MARIAVITE CHURCH

THE Mariavite Church of Poland had its origin within the Roman Catholic Church as a community of nuns for the perpetual adoration of the Blessed Sacrament founded by Maria Frances Kozlowska, who claimed to have been the recipient of a series of revelations. This community was connected with an order of priests observing the Franciscan rule. Various irregularities were alleged against them, and they were condemned at Rome, mainly through the influence of the Jesuits, and excommunicated.

In 1908 the leaders of this body were introduced to the Old Catholic bishops by the Russian theologian, General Alexander Kireef. The Old Catholic bishops admitted them to communion, and in 1910 Jean Marie Kowalski was consecrated bishop for them by Archbishop Gul. For a time the Mariavite Church flourished considerably, but it has since declined, and no doubt suffered greatly during the recent war.

During the first world war, and in the years that followed, the Mariavite Church fell into grave irregularities, with the ordination of women and other offences against Catholic custom. The first Archbishop was then expelled, and two priests and seventy nuns went with him. His sect has now practically died out. Other irregularities began after the death of the foundress, when Archbishop Michael Kowalski claimed himself as inspired, to be incapable of sin and so on. Later this took extreme forms; he claimed that the Mariavites were the Kingdom of God on earth, and he used this to introduce moral anarchy. He was later sent to prison for sedition by the Polish Government. In 1924 the Archbishop of Utrecht, on discovering these errors, severed communion with the body.

At the outbreak of the late war there were five bishops of the Church, with a certain Philip Feldman as Archbishop. The headquarters of the movement at that time was at Płock. There is a Bishop Fatome in France who is a Mariavite bishop, and a certain 'Archbishop Matthew' in England who also claims to be such; there are also one or two English persons who claim to be Mariavite priests.

In the autumn of 1946 the Mariavite Church formed a union with the so-called 'Old Catholic Church of Poland', another Polish body not in communion with the See of Utrecht. The two bodies have agreed to pool their resources, while each will retain its own organization and doctrinal teaching. Bishop Prysiecki of the Old Catholic Church of Poland is to be head of the new sect, with Bishop Faron as his assistant and the Mariavite Bishop Zygmunt Szypopold, as second assistant.

CHAPTER IX

BISHOP LOUIS CHARLES WINNAERT

THE case of Bishop Louis Charles Winnaert demands some notice here, although he has left no succession, and his following is now united with the Moscow Patriarchate and under the Exarch in Paris.

In 1905 Winnaert was ordained priest in the Roman Catholic Church, but he became a Modernist, and withdrew from the Roman Communion, with a small following, in 1918. He approached Dr. Bury, Anglican Bishop in Northern and Central Europe, with a view to being received into the Anglican Church and subsequently consecrated bishop. This request was refused, but Bishop Bury put a small church at his disposal, in which he ministered for a short time, and he also apparently had leave to hold services in French in St. George's Anglican church in Paris. In 1921 he was ministering as an Old Catholic priest at St. Denis, with the permission of Dr. Gul, Archbishop of Utrecht. He left Dr. Gul, however, in 1922, as a result of various differences between them, and later in the same year his followers formed themselves into an independent Modernist body, styled the 'Eglise catholique libre', of which they elected Winnaert bishop. He then approached Bishop Wedgwood of the Liberal Catholic Church, and from him received consecration. In 1930 he appears to have had parishes in Paris, Brussels, Rouen, Holland and Rome. After 1930 the term 'Eglise catholique évangélique' was used.

In 1931 or 1932 he approached the Metropolitan Evlogie with a view to being received into the Orthodox Church, together with his congregations. The Metropolitan Evlogie referred the matter to the Œcumenical Patriarchate, which did not accede to his request that his movement be received as a Western Rite, but insisted upon them adopting the Eastern Rite, which Winnaert was unwilling to do. He then approached the Metropolitan Sergius of Moscow, who directed Bishop Elefthery of Latvia to receive him and his congregations. He was received in January 1937, and, his episcopal orders being declared doubtful at Moscow, was received as a priest. He applied for consecration as bishop, but, this being denied him, was assigned the rank of Archimandrite. He died on March 3rd of the same year. His followers may now be found in Paris in three communities. One is a parish using the Roman Rite with some modifications; another is a parish using in a revised form the Rite of the Eglise catholique évangélique; the third is an Orthodox Benedictine monastery. All three are now under the Moscow Patriarchate, but the two first are also under Constantinople. Whatever may be thought of Winnaert's judgment, his personal character was without blemish.

"Winnaert was a Modernist of the second rank," writes Professor Robert P. Casey. "Possessing neither the speculative power of Tyrell nor the erudition of Loisy and his associates, he was more uncompromising than they in the original Modernist purpose of producing a church, a living community which was both liberal in theology and traditional in sentiment and culture. . . . Experience has unfortunately shown that so tenuous a grasp of theology is ill adapted to popular demands and incapable of sustaining the weight of a large organization. It is significant that Winnaert saved the religious life of his scattered groups by radical compromises with the kind of orthodoxy he had at first repudiated."[1]

[1] Art. 'Transient Cults' in *Psychiatry*, vol. IV, p. 527.

CHAPTER X

DR. F. G. LEE AND THE ORDER OF CORPORATE REUNION

THE generally accepted story of this movement[1] is that in the summer of 1877 two Anglican clergymen, Dr. F. G. Lee, Vicar of All Saints', Lambeth, and T. W. Mossman, Rector of Torrington in the diocese of Lincoln, together with a Dr. John T. Seccombe, a Norfolk medical man and a magistrate, went to Venice, and near that city, in a boat, were conditionally re-baptized, confirmed, ordained deacon and priest, and consecrated bishop, by a mysterious triumvirate of a Greek, a Coptic and a Roman Catholic (or Jansenist) Bishop. The reason for this movement appears to have been less a disbelief in the validity of Anglican Orders—of which Dr. Lee had written a learned defence in 1869—than a desire to provide the Church of England with a succession which Rome would be compelled to recognize as valid. The three bishops styled themselves Bishop of Dorchester (Lee), Caerleon (Seccombe) and Selby (Mossman). It has been asserted[2] that they re-ordained as many as six or eight hundred Anglican clergy, and while this number is an undoubted exaggeration, there is reason to believe that the number was considerable. The names of the consecrating prelates were never divulged to the public, and were communicated to those intending to join the Order only under the seal of the Confessional. There seems to be no doubt that the Orders were accepted as valid at the Vatican, and Lee preserved a document, which has been seen by a number of persons still living, giving some sort of Papal recognition of their validity.

The generally accepted story, however, does not appear to be accurate on all points. A letter exists, written in 1862 by Seccombe and signed with a cross as a bishop. Seccombe

[1] As told, for example, in Walsh's *Secret History of the Oxford Movement*; in the article on Lee in the *Dictionary of National Biography*; in G. J. Slosser's *Christian Unity* and in many contemporary newspaper and periodical accounts; it is partly accepted by Canon S. L. Ollard in several of his books.

[2] Notably by Walter Walsh in *The Secret History*. . . .

was later connected with Ferrete, and it is just possible that he had some sort of Syrian Orders, or at any rate claimed them. There is strong circumstantial evidence for the belief that the consecrator of Mossman was either the Archbishop of Milan himself or, more probably, some prelate connected with that See. Lee was probably consecrated at, or near, Venice, possibly by the Bishop of Murano or, more probably, by an Armenian prelate connected with the Mekhitarists on the Island of San Lazzaro at Venice. In any case, it is almost certain that the consecrators of Lee and Mossman were prelates in communion with Rome. The original Order of Corporate Reunion was a complete failure and was strongly repudiated by High Churchmen.[1]

It is not known certainly whether Lee has left a succession; the whole proceedings of the Order were shrouded in secrecy, and the few papers which Lee left on the subject were destroyed by his son, the late Mr. Ambrose Lee. It is very unlikely, however, that any of the O.C.R. bishops performed a consecration, though Lee and Mossman assisted at the consecration of Stevens of the Ferrete succession. Prelates have, however, arisen claiming to be bishops of the original Order of Corporate Reunion, and there has been no means of checking the truth of their claim, though since they would be unable to reveal the ultimate source of their Orders, they could not be accepted as validly consecrated. For a number of years there flourished a curious prelate in South London called Richard C. Jackson, who styled himself 'Richard, Archprelate of the O.C.R.'. Jackson was certainly at one time connected with Lee, and was Prior of a somewhat amateur monastery founded by George Nugee in the Old Kent Road. He was a man of some culture, and was a F.R.Hist.S. and a vice-president of the Dante Society; a friend of Walter Pater, he claimed to be Pater's inspiration for the romance *Marius the Epicurean*. There is considerable doubt as to whether Jackson was ever a bishop at all, though it is possible that he was consecrated by Benedict Donkin. In any case it is unlikely that he was consecrated by one of the original O.C.R. prelates. He died in 1937.

J. C. Whitebrook, brother of the William Whitebrook of the Ferrete succession, claimed to be an O.C.R. bishop, but we have seen no evidence to substantiate the claim, though the brothers Whitebrook were certainly at one time attached to Lee's church as servers.

[1] See, e.g., *Statement of the Society of the Holy Cross concerning the Order of Corporate Reunion.*

CHAPTER XI

ANTHONY ANEED

ANTHONY ANEED was originally a Melkite priest, and secretary to Archbishop Athanasius Sawaya of Beyrouth, Syria. Thereafter he migrated to America and served a Melkite parish in New York. In 1911 Archbishop Sawaya was refused permission by the Pope to visit America, but, disobeying the papal prohibition, he sailed for the United States, and made his home for a time with Aneed. Aneed claims, and supports his claim with certain documents, that Sawaya then consecrated him, in a private chapel, as Auxiliary Bishop of the Archdiocese of Beyrouth, and confirmed him in his office as Exarch of the Archbishop for the Melkites in the United States.

Aneed appears to have suppressed all claims to this episcopate from 1911 until about 1942, but he has now completely severed connection with Rome, and formed what he is pleased to call the 'Byzantine American Church'. This body was incorporated in California in 1944. Aneed has a Syrian congregation in, or near, San Francisco. In a circular announcing the consecration of O. A. Barry (see p. 68), Aneed is described as 'Patriarch-President, Federated Independent Catholic and Orthodox Churches'.

In 1945 Aneed, assisted by Kleefisch, Wadle and Verostek, consecrated a certain Frank B. Robinson. Robinson was an occultist and head of the 'Psychiana Society' of Moscow, Idaho, and he appears to have continued in this position after his consecration.[1]

[1] An article on Robinson entitled 'The Archbishop seeks Gold' was printed in the American *Frauds and Answers Magazine* for April, 1945.

CHAPTER XII

UNCLASSIFIED *EPISCOPI VAGANTES*

THERE are several stray *episcopi vagantes* whose antecedents are doubtful and who appear to be independent of the main lines of succession.

There is a strange body in the West Indies, which describes itself simply as 'The Orthodox Church', of which 'His Eminence E. M. Jack' is called 'The International Exalted Archbishop in Charge'. In one of the publications of this body it is stated that the "bishopric of the Episcopal Orthodox Church" was established on September 23rd, 1923, but no information is given as to the source of his supposed episcopal Orders. The sect has a small following, entirely black, in Barbados and Trinidad.

A prelate who appeared in 1932 was one 'Mar Silwa, Archbishop of Nineveh'. He has since disappeared, and nothing seems to be known either about him or his credentials.

Stephen Theodosius de Nemeth claimed to have been consecrated by the Jacobite Patriarch Ignatius Ephrem I on September 23rd, 1934, as first Archbishop of the 'Greek Oriental Hungarian Orthodox Church'. There appears to be no doubt that de Nemeth was validly consecrated at Homs by the Syrian Patriarch, but from such information as is available it appears that his approach to the Patriarch was motivated by a desire to obtain episcopal Orders, and so to form a Church. Presumably his followers consist of a few people who have broken away from one of the two Orthodox jurisdictions in Hungary dependent either upon the Œcumenical Patriarchate or the Serb Patriarchate. Stefan Boros, originally a priest of the American Catholic Church, claims to be a Bishop of the 'Hungarian Greek Catholic Church' in New York. There is no information as to the source of his orders, but they may derive from de Nemeth.

An American sect is the 'Apostolic Episcopal Church', whose bishop is Arthur Wolfort Brooks. In *The Year Book of American Churches* it claims 2639 members and 19 churches, while in the same publication it describes itself as "a body which acknowledges the historic Eastern Confession and Order. It claims apostolic orders through the Chaldean succession, and was constituted in 1925 by the consecration of its first bishop". Two different statements appear to exist as to Brooks' consecration: in one place it is stated that he was "elevated to the episcopate by Bishop Antoine, Archpresbyter James and Archdeacon Evodius of the Chaldean Church, on May 4th, 1925". Another document states that he was received into the Eastern Church by the titular Bishop of Iconium and the titular Bishop of Tarsus."[1] It is by no means clear who these various persons may be; the Chaldean Uniates, from whom it is claimed the succession is derived, have a small colony of some 750 persons in America with one or two priests, but no bishop. In a little tract issued by Brooks he claims that his church was instituted "by canonical authority, by representation and delegation from the Patriarch of the Chaldean Church". This does not seem probable. Brooks appears to have some connection with the revived Ferrete succession which has accorded him the title of 'Titular Archbishop of Ebbsfleet'.[2] In 1933 a certain William H. Du Bois was listed as a bishop and officer of his sect, and on September 16th, 1934, Brooks consecrated two bishops: Charles William Keller and Harold F. Jarvis, the rite used being that of the Chaldean Uniates. Brooks at one time claimed connection with G. W. Plummer, but this was denied by Plummer.

A further American sect is the 'Old Roman Catholic Apostolic Church', under a Bishop Michael d'Ielsi, a former Roman Catholic priest who appears to have been consecrated by one of the Vilatte bishops and who works among poor Italians in New York State. His body is said to have a membership of some 2500.

Henry J. Kleefisch claims to have been consecrated in 1918 at Harbin by Archbishop Sergius, later Patriarch of Moscow, and two other fugitive bishops, under a 'Canon of Necessity'. He later migrated to America and is now a practising lawyer in San Francisco. He is an apostle of what is called, in America, 'The Truth Movement', which appears to be a degenerate type of Theosophy.

A certain Raymundo O'Donnell claims to be 'Supreme Bishop' of the 'Iglesia Independista de la Santisima Trinidad de Filipinas', and to have been consecrated in 1935. It appears, however, that he received no consecration whatever.

Francis Lashley is a New York coloured bishop and titular head of a body he organized called 'the American

[1] From a statement in the files of the Advisory Commission on Ecclesiastical Relations of the Protestant Episcopal Church.

[2] *Orthodox Catholic Review*, June, 1944.

Catholic Church of New York', but which appears to have no connection with, or continuity from, the Vilatte-Lloyd American Catholic Church. He was possibly consecrated by Tyarchs.

Stephen Geniotis is a Lithuanian who was ordained priest in 1916 by de Landas, and he remained a priest under Carfora until 1928. He then resigned, and appeared as 'Bishop' Geniotis of the 'Catholic Church of America'. He later claimed to have been consecrated in 1924 or 1925 by de Landas, but as de Landas died in 1920, this claim makes it probable that he has received no consecration whatever. In 1933 Bishop Crummey of the Universal Episcopal Communion issued a *Bulletin of Information upon the Ecclesiastical Status of one Stephen Geniotis, a suspended Priest of the North American Old Roman Catholic Church.*

John Styles claimed to have been ordained priest by Vilatte. Later he called himself 'Archbishop' Styles, and has his own independent church in Los Angeles, but there is no authenticated information as to who consecrated him.

One who is at least a potential *episcopus vagans* has appeared in Brazil. He is Mgr. Duarte, Roman Catholic Bishop of Maura, who in June, 1945, was excommunicated by the Pope, after initiating a strongly anti-Papal campaign on the grounds of supposed alliance between the Vatican and Fascism. Mgr. Duarte has announced that he intends setting up his own 'Brazilian Catholic Apostolic Church', a title the shape of which has a familiar ring. On August 15th, 1945, he gave "solene investidura da 'sacra episcopalis' " [consecration?] to Saloměo Ferraz of the 'Igreja Católica Livre no Brasil'. This body appears to have been organized in 1936 and to have elected Ferraz bishop. Faron, a Polish old Catholic bishop not recognized by Utrecht, offered to consecrate him, but this was found impossible owing to distances. He called himself 'Bishop' Ferraz on the strength, apparently, of his election. Further information concerning his movement will be found in *O Estado de São Paulo*, notably in the issues for January 2nd and 6th, 1938, and in Ferraz' book *A Fé Nacional.*

Odo Acheson Barry was consecrated on July 29th, 1946, as "Bishop of the Dominion of Canada, Canadian Catholic Church". The consecrator was Charles Hampton of the Liberal Catholic Church, assisted by Wadle, Aneed, Strange and Kleefisch. The consecration took place in California and the Canadian body is affiliated with the American Catholic Church under Wadle.

APPENDIX A

Notice from the Syrian Patriarchate of Antioch and All the East

The Syrian Orthodox Patriarchate of Antioch and all the East proclaims to all whom it may concern that there are in the United States of America and in some countries of Europe, particularly in England, a number of schismatic bodies which have come into existence after direct expulsion from official Christian communities and have devised for themselves a common creed and system of jurisdiction of their own invention.

To deceive Christians of the West being a chief objective of the schismatic bodies, they take advantage of their great distance from the East, and from time to time make public statements claiming without truth to derive their origin and apostolic succession from some ancient Apostolic Church of the East, the attractive rites and ceremonies of which they adopt and with which they claim to have relationship.

Since (as, for example, the so-called 'One Holy Orthodox Catholic Church' as it describes itself, presided over, as it is claimed, by the so-called Frederic Harrington, 'Metropolitan' in the city of London, of 324, Hornsey Road, and all the sects claiming succession through Vilatte, namely, the American Catholic Church, the Polish Catholic Church, the National Orthodox Church of America, the African Orthodox Church, etc., and others) some of these schismatic bodies have with effrontery published statements which are untrue as to an alleged relation 'in succession and ordination' to our Holy Apostolic Church and her forefathers, We find it necessary to announce to all whom it may concern that we deny any and every relation whatsoever with these schismatic bodies and repudiate them and their claims absolutely. Furthermore, our Church forbids any and every relationship and, above all, intercommunion with all and any of these schismatic sects and warns the public that their statements and pretensions as above are altogether without truth.

SEAL OF THE SYRIAN
PATRIARCHATE OF ANTIOCH
HOMS.

Homs, December 10, 1938.

APPENDIX B

SELECTED BIBLIOGRAPHY

THE MATHEW SUCCESSION

The Direct Succession

Archbishop of Canterbury, the, and Bishop Matheu. N.P., 1915.

Articles of Belief of the Old Catholics in Great Britain and Ireland, of the Western Orthodox Church. Bromley, 1911.

Bell, G. K. A., *Randall Davidson*, ch. lxiii.

British Uniate Rite, A. By an Old Roman Catholic Priest. Stroud, N.D.

Catholic Standard, The. Bromley, 1911. Only a few numbers issued.

Mathew, A. H., *The Old Catholic Missal and Ritual.* London, 1909.

Are Anglican Orders Valid? London, 1910.

The Catholic Church of England: Its Constitution, Faith, Episcopal Succession, etc. Bromley, 1914.

A Catechism of Christian Doctrine. Bromley, 1914.

Pastoral Letter on Membership in the Theosophical Society and in the Order of the Star of the East. N.P. or D.

The Ancient Catholic Church of Great Britain and Ireland. N.P. or D.

An Episcopal Odyssey. Privately printed. Kingsdown, 1915.

Old Catholic Almanack and Guide, The. Stroud, 1926ff.

Reveil Catholique, Le: Organe de l'Eglise catholique française. Paris, 1914.

Torch, The: A Monthly Review advocating the Reconstruction of the Church of the West and Reunion with the Holy Orthodox Church of the East. Acton, 1912.

Union Review, The. Bromley, 1913. Only three issues published.

Wedgwood, J. I., *The Lambeth Conference and the Validity of Archbishop Mathew's Orders:* An Open Letter to his Grace the Archbishop of Canterbury. Sydney, N.D.

Williams, B. M., *What is an Old Roman Catholic?* N.P. 1920.

A Pastoral Letter for Advent, 1920. N.P. 1920.

A Summary of the History, Faith, Discipline and Aims of the Old Roman Catholic Church in Great Britain. Stroud, 1924.

The English Text of the Ordinary of the Mass for Use in the Old Roman Catholic Church in Great Britain. Stroud, 1924.

The History and Purpose of the Old Roman Catholic (Pro-Uniate) Rite in Great Britain. Gloucester, 1939.

Bishop Howarth

Howarth, A. W., *A Protest against the Tyranny of the Roman Inquisition and of His Holiness Pope Pius X.* Privately printed. 1919.

Bishop Banks

The Independent Catholic Church: Its Constitution, etc. By James, Patriarch of Windsor. Sutton Bridge, 1922.

Banks, J. B., *The Pontifical of the Independent Catholic Church.* Sutton Bridge, 1922.

A Broad Statement of the Principles and Facts of the Independent Catholic Church. Privately printed, 1924.
The Service Church: Its Constitution, etc. London, 1925.

AMERICAN SUCCESSION: BROTHERS

The Story of the Old Catholic Church in America. Cos Cob. N.D.

AMERICAN SUCCESSION: CARFORA

The Catholic American. Official Publication of the Holy Catholic Church in America. Chicago, 1925. [Carfora & Lloyd.]
Brief of the Life of the Most Rev. Carmel Henry Carfora. N.P. or D.
Carfora, C. H., *General Constitution and Bye-Laws of the North American Old Roman Catholic Church.* New York, N.D.
Vanderfil, H. J., *Explanation of the Present Position of the Old Catholics in the World.* Chicago, 1919.
American National Catholic, the: Official Quarterly Bulletin of the North American Old Roman Catholic Church. Chicago, 1944ff.

THE LIBERAL CATHOLIC CHURCH

Leadbeater, C. W., *The Science of the Sacraments.* Adyar, 1929.
Liberal Catholic Church, the: Statement of Principles, Summary of Doctrine and Table of Apostolic Succession. London, 5th ed., 1938.
Pigott, F. W., *Catholicism—Past and Future.* London, N.D.

WHITMAN

Whitman, R., *An Open Letter to the British Old Catholics.* Gloucester, 1940.

BISHOP WINNAERT

Winnaert, L. C., *Le Problème de l'Unité chrétienne.* Paris, 1924.
Winnaert, L. C., *Quelques Mots sur l'Orthodoxie adressés à des Occidentaux.* Paris, 1944.

THE VILATTE SUCCESSION

ARCHBISHOP VILATTE

Church Review, the, October, 1898–January, 1899.
de Angelis, A., *A Friendly Correction of the Rev. A. Parker Curtiss' Statements about Father Vilatte in the Holy Cross Magazine for August, 1920.* Chicago, 1920.
Parisot, J., *Monseigneur Vilatte: Fondateur de l'Eglise vieille-catholique au Etats-Unis d'Amerique.* Tours & Mayenne, 1899.
Recent Ordination of Father Ignatius at Llanthony Abbey. Reprinted from the *Hereford Times.* London, 1898.
Vilatte, J. R., *The Independent Catholic Movement in France.* London, 1907.
Mode of Receiving the Profession of the Old Catholic Faith from one Newly Converted. Chicago, 1919.
William, Bro., O.S.B., *The Genesis of Old Catholicism in America.* Buffalo (1898).

THE VILATTE SUCCESSION; AMERICA.

American Churchman, the: Official Publication of the American Catholic Church. Chicago, 1928ff.
Lines, G., *The American Catholic Church: What it is. Where it came from. What it stands for.* Los Angeles. N.D.

Liturgy, the, according to the Use of the American Catholic Church (Western-Orthodox) in the Province of the Pacific. N.P. or D.

THE VILATTE SUCCESSION: ENGLAND

Catholic Christian, the: A Magazine of the Catholic Christian Church (Stannard). Bournemouth, 1934. One number only.

Harrington, F. C. A., *The Apostolic Succession of the One, Holy Orthodox-Catholic Church.* London (1938).

The Orthodox-Keltic Rite of Ordination of Deacons and Priests. London (1939).

The Christian Doctrine of the Theandric Final Life. London (1938).

Herbert, D., *The Jesuene Church.* Abergavenny (1937).

The Free Orthodox-Catholic Apostolic Succession. N.P. or D.

Women Priesthood. Abergavenny (1943).

Ignatius Redivivus: Llanthony Atmosphere at Abergavenny. Reprinted from the *Abergavenny Chronicle*, May 1st, 1942. Abergavenny, 1942.

Old Catholics and the Vicar of Branksome. [Parkstone], 1918.

Picturesque Ceremony at Abergavenny, a: Consecration of a Bishop. (F. D. Bacon.) Abergavenny, N.D.

Sibley, C., *The Syrian Rite of the Holy Eucharist abridged.* London, 1929.

Statement of the Primary Doctrines and Principles of the Catholic Christian Church. (Stannard.) Bournemouth, 1933.

Statement concerning the Church, Sacraments and Worship of the Catholic Christian Church. Bournemouth, 1933.

Ward, J. S. M., *The Orthodox Catholic Church in England.* New Barnet. (1936.)

The Liturgy of the Orthodox Catholic Church in England. New Barnet. (1936.)

Whitebrook, W., *The Independent Catholics of Great Britain.* London, N.D.

AFRICAN ORTHODOX CHURCH

African Orthodox Churchman, the. Beaconsfield. 1932ff.

Alexander, D. W., *Constitution and Canons and Episcopate of the African Orthodox Church.* Beaconsfield, 1942.

The Onward Movement in Preparation for the 10th Annual Synod. Beaconsfield. 1934.

Negro Churchman, the. Published in the Interest of the African Orthodox Church. New York, 1923ff.

THE FERRETE SUCCESSION

Catholic Apostolic Church, the: A Statement for Candid Enquirers. Glastonbury, 1946.

Ancient Christian Fellowship Review, the. [Ottega-Maxey], Los Angeles, 1946—.

Encyclical Letter of the Holy Governing Synod of the Catholicate of the West Concerning the Extension of the Catholicate to the Americas. N.P., 1946.

Ferrete, J., *Euchologion: The Eastern Liturgy adapted for Use in the West.* Oxford & London, 1866.

Hayman, V. A. P., *Catholic Freedom: A Brief Summary of the Position and Outlook of the Free Catholic Church.* London, 1930.

Langhelt, F. E. (Ed.), *A Chapter of Secret History*, reprinted by kind permission of the *Church Times* from its issue of April 28th, 1922, page 445, with sundry Notes not forming part of the original Article. Glastonbury, 1945.

Newman, H. G. de W., *The Old Catholic Orthodox Church: General Information.* Northampton, 1942.

Pastoral Letter of His Beatitude Mar Georgius on the Occasion of his Consecration. London, 1944.

Pastoral Letter of His Beatitude Mar Georgius for Advent, 1945. London, 1945.

Orthodox Catholic Leaflet: I. *Table of Apostolic Succession in the Western Orthodox Catholic Church.*

II. *Historical Notes concerning the Western Orthodox Catholic Church.* London, 1944.

III. *The Restoration of Apostolic Catholicism.* Glastonbury, N.D.

IV. *Table of Apostolic Succession (Armenian-Uniate Line).* Glastonbury, 1945.

V. *Table of Apostolic Succession (Old Catholic Line from America)*

Orthodox Catholic Review, the. Enfield Lock. 1944ff.

Patriarchate of Antioch: Ancient Orthodox Catholic Church. (Crow.) N.P. or D.

THE ORDER OF CORPORATE REUNION

Lee, F. G., 'The Order of Corporate Reunion' in the *Nineteenth Century,* November, 1881.

'The O.C.R. and its Work' in the *Nineteenth Century,* November, 1898

Livius, T., C.SS.R., *The Order of Corporate Reunion.* Dublin, 1882.

Pastoral Letter of the Rector, Provincials and Provosts of the Order of Corporate Reunion, September 8th, 1877. London, 1877.

Reunion Magazine, the. London, 1877–79. Four numbers only issued.

Statement of the Society of the Holy Cross concerning the Order of Corporate Reunion. London, 1879.

Vernon Herford

Herford, V., *Pastoral Letter of . . . to the Syro-Chaldeans of the Metropolitan See of India, Milapur, Ceylon, etc.* Oxford, 1903.

Autobiographical Note on the Rt. Rev. Bishop Vernon Herford. Issued with the S.U.P.P.C.A. Report for 1937. N.P. 1937.

Evangelical Catholic Communion Leaflets: I–X. Oxford, v.d.

The Church and Chapel Parish Magazine. Oxford, 1929–30.

Apostolic Episcopal Church

An Act to amend the Religious Corporations Law, in Relation to Incorporation of Apostolic Episcopal Parishes or Churches. Senate of the State of New York, 1932.

Brooks, A. W., *Apostolic Episcopal Church.* New York. (1930.)

Ecclesia, the. New York, 1943.

Ecclesiastical Letters of Recognition of the Rt. Rev. A. W. Brooks by the Congregation of Christ's Church by the Sea, Broad Channel, New York City. New York, 1930.

Raymundo O'Donnell

Iglesia Independista de la Santisima Trinidad de Filipinas. Manila, 1935.

APPENDIX C

LIST OF THE PRINCIPAL CHURCHES AND ORGANIZATIONS PRESIDED OVER BY EPISCOPI VAGANTES [1]

MATHEW SUCCESSION

Old Roman Catholic (Pro-Uniate) Rite of Great Britain (B. M. Williams).
North American Old Roman Catholic Church (C. H. Carfora).
Universal Episcopal Communion (J. C. Crummey).
Universal Christian Communion (J. C. Crummey).
Liberal Catholic Church (F. W. Pigott).
Old Catholic Church in America (W. H. F. Brothers).
Mexican Old Roman Catholic Church (J. P. Ortiz).
Protestant Orthodox Western Church (H. A. Rogers).
Independent Catholic Church (J. B. Banks).
The Sanctuary (F. James).

VILATTE SUCCESSION

American Catholic Church (L. P. Wadle).
African Orthodox Church (two factions, presided over by R. A. Valentine and W. E. Robertson respectively).
Free Orthodox Catholic Church (D. Herbert).
African Universal Church (E. J. Anderson).
Communion Evangelica Catholica Eucharistica (F. Heiler). Gallican Church (L. F. Giraud).

FERRETE SUCCESSION

Orthodox Catholic Church (H. G. de W. Newman).
Order of the Holy Wisdom (W. B. Crow).
Free Protestant Church of England (G. Pinder).
Free Protestant Church (W. Hall).

UNCLASSIFIED

Evangelical Catholic Communion (W. J. E. Jeffery).
North American Orthodox Church (A. Tyler Turner).
Mariavite Church of Poland (Philip Feldman).
Apostolic Episcopal Church (A. W. Brooks).
Anglican Universal Church (J. R. C. Toombes).
Old Roman Catholic Apostolic Church (M. d'Ielsi).
Greek Oriental Hungarian Orthodox Church (S. T. de Nemeth).
Byzantine American Church (A. Aneed).
Independent Church of the Holy Trinity of the Philippines (R. O'Donnell).
American Catholic Church of New York (F. Lashley).
Apostolic Polish Church of Canada (P. A. R. Markiewicz).
Igreja Católica Livre no Brasil (S. Ferraz).

[1] Names in brackets indicate the present head of each organization. It should be emphasized that the majority of these are paper organizations only.

INDEX

www.ingramcontent.com/pod-product-compliance
Lightning Source LLC
LaVergne TN
LVHW050934080826
845145LV00004B/1250

* 9 7 8 0 9 7 7 1 4 6 1 7 8 *